Tales of the Forbidden City

Edited by Cheng Qinhua

Foreign Languages Press

First Edition 1997
Second Printing 1998

ISBN 7-119-01742-X

© Foreign Languages Press, Beijing, China, 1997

Published by Foreign Languages Press
24 Baiwanzhuang Road, Beijing 100037, China

Distributed by China International Book Trading Corporation
35 Chegongzhuang Xilu, Beijing 100044, China
P.O. Box 399, Beijing, China

Printed in the People's Republic of China

Contents

Foreword   1

Chapter One
Brief Introduction to the Forbidden City   3
  1. A Sea of Regal Buildings   3
  2. The Construction of the Forbidden City   4
  3. The Layout of the Forbidden City   4
  4. Why Is It Called the Forbidden City?   5
  5. Manpower for the Construction   5
  6. Sightseeing Routes in the Forbidden City   6

Chapter Two
The Main Structures in the Forbidden City   9
  1. The Meridian Gate—Main Entrance to the Forbidden
    City   9
  2. Inner Golden Stream—A Splendid Man-Made River   10
  3. The Gate of Supreme Harmony—Where the Emperor
    Discharged His Official Duties   11
  4. The Hall of Supreme Harmony—Where Grand Imperial
    Ceremonies Were Held   12
  5. The Hall of Central Harmony—Where the Emperor
    Rested Before Grand Ceremonies   15
  6. The Hall of Preserving Harmony—Where the Highest-
    Level Civil Service Examination Was Held   16
  7. The Gate of Heavenly Purity—Entrance to the Quarters
    of the Imperial Household   17
  8. The Palace of Heavenly Purity—Living Quarters of the
    Emperor   18
  9. The Hall of Celestial and Terrestrial Union   20
  10. The Palace of Earthly Tranquility—Nuptial Chamber of
     the Emperor and Empress   21

11. The Imperial Garden—Leisure Park of the Imperial
    Household   22
12. The Six Western Palaces—Living Quarters of the
    Imperial Household   24
13. The Six Eastern Palaces—Treasure Stores of Art   28
14. The Palace of Tranquil Longevity—A Little Forbidden
    City Within the Forbidden City   30

Chapter Three

Insights into the Imperial Lifestyle   36

1. The Emperor's Diet and the Palace Cuisine   36
2. The Emperor's Grand Nuptials   38
3. The Selection of the Palace Harem and Lives of
   Concubines in the Inner Palace   43
4. How Did an Empress Bathe?   45
5. Where Were the Toilets?   46
6. Where Did the Water Come from   47
7. Keeping Warm and Cool   47
8. The Six Big Fires in the Forbidden City   48
9. Palace Ladies Try to Assassinate the Emperor   50
10. Foreign Artists at the Qing Court   51
11. Foreigner Records the Inauguration of the Imperial
    Palace   52
12. The Attempted Murder of a Crown Prince   54
13. An Heir-Apparent Raised in Secret   54
14. "The Cricket Emperor"   56
15. The Empress Dowager Marries the Emperor's Uncle   56
16. How Emperor Kangxi Removed Aobai   57
17. Mystery of How Yongzheng Became Emperor   58
18. Cixi's Wealth and Her Extravagance in Dining   59
19. Cixi Intercedes for the Empress   61
20. The Empress Dowager's Cruelty   62
21. Friction Between the East Empress Dowager and the
    West Empress Dowager   63
22. The Tragedy of Concubine Zhen   65

23. Anecdotes of the Last Emperor   66
24. Connotations of the Motifs on the Imperial Robe and the *Bufu*   67
25. How Many Rooms Are There in the Forbidden City?   70
26. Corner Towers of the Forbidden City   70
27. Stage Plays in the Imperial Palace   71
28. The Bronze Lions of the Forbidden City   72
29. The Bronze Vats for Fire Protection   73
30. What Is the Significance of the Number of the Gate Nails?   73
31. Mosaics in the Imperial Garden   74

Chapter Four
The 24 Ming and Qing Emperors Who Lived in the Forbidden City

    75
1. Emperor Chengzu—Zhu Di (1360-1424)   75
2. Emperor Renzong—Zhu Gaochi (1378-1425)   78
3. Emperor Xuanzong—Zhu Zhanji (1398-1435)   79
4. Emperor Yingzong—Zhu Qizhen (1427-1464)   80
5. Emperor Daizong—Zhu Qiyu (1428-1457)   82
6. Emperor Xianzong—Zhu Jianshen (1447-1487)   83
7. Emperor Xiaozong—Zhu Youcheng (1470-1505)   84
8. Emperor Wuzong—Zhu Houzhao (1491-1521)   86
9. Emperor Shizong—Zhu Houcong (1507-1566)   88
10. Emperor Muzong—Zhu Zaihou (1537-1572)   90
11. Emperor Shenzong—Zhu Yijun (1563-1620)   91
12. Emperor Guangzong—Zhu Changluo (1585-1620)   92
13. Emperor Xizong—Zhu Youxiao (1605-1627)   93
14. Emperor Sizong—Zhu Youjian (1611-1644)   95
15. Emperor Shizu—Fu Lin (1638-1661)   96
16. Emperor Shengzu—Xuan Ye (1654-1722)   98
17. Emperor Shizong—Yin Zhen (1678-1735)   100
18. Emperor Gaozong—Hong Li (1711-1799)   101
19. Emperor Renzong—Yong Yan (1760-1820)   104
20. Emperor Xuanzong—Min Ning (1782-1850)   105

21. Emperor Wenzong—Yi Zhu (1831-1861) 108
22. Emperor Muzong—Zai Chun (1856-1875) 110
23. Emperor Dezong—Zai Tian (1871-1908) 111
24. The Last Emperor—Pu Yi (1906-1967) 113

Appendix
1. Emperors of the Ming Dynasty 116
2. Emperors of the Qing Dynasty 117

Foreword

The Forbidden City, also known as the Imperial Palace, is located in the center of Beijing. It is the largest ancient palace in the world, with clusters of well-preserved buildings. From early in the morning thousands of tourists from all over China and abroad swarm into the Palace to view its magnificent halls and priceless treasures.

On my way to my office I like cycling along the outside of the wall of the Forbidden City. In the early morning sunshine I ride from the Eastern Flowery Gate (Donghuamen) to the path between the lofty wall of the Forbidden City and the moat outside the Eastern Palace Gate (Donggongmen) and pedal northward. When I reach the watchtower in the northeast corner of the Palace I turn the corner and go west along the riverside, verdant with weeping willows. After work I cycle home along the same route. I have lost count of how many times I have been to the Forbidden City. As an editor, I have got to know many specialists in cultural relics who work in the Palace, and several have become good friends of mine. When we meet we often talk animatedly about the changes in the Forbidden City and the treasures housed in it. I am an avid reader of historical materials concerning the Palace and the history of the Ming and Qing dynasties. This has gradually enabled me to know more about this magnificent yet mysterious edifice, and has prompted me to write this book about it.

Works concerning the Forbidden City are so numerous that it is quite impossible for an ordinary reader to read all of them. Therefore, in this book I concentrate on describing the buildings and the residents' lives in a straightforward language. It is a tale of savage intrigue and power struggles among the splendid buildings, resplendent with the fascinating pageantry of the imperial court. The actors are real-life emperors, ministers, generals and concu-

1

bines. You will also be introduced to famous spots of historical interest, and the fabulous treasures stored in the Palace, and their stories.... All these accounts are helpful for those who are interested in the history of the Ming and Qing dynasties and the life of the imperial household. Some of the historical materials and research essays quoted in this book are the results of the painstaking work of scholars of several generations. All I have done is sorted out historical materials, edited them and presented them in a new way.

Chapter One
Brief Introduction to the Forbidden City

1. A Sea of Regal Buildings

Gazing for the first time on the countless red walls and bright yellow glazed-tile roofs of the buildings of the Forbidden City, one cannot help wondering exactly how large the Palace is. To be exact, it is 960 m long from south to north, and 750 m wide from east to west, occupying 720,000 sq m. The total floor area is 160,000 sq m and there are 9,999 rooms. (According to Chinese custom, a "room" refers to a space within four pillars.)

How long and how high is the perimeter wall of the Forbidden City? It is 3,400 m long and 10 m high. The moat outside the Palace is 3,800 m long and 52 m wide. The moat was built for security purposes, and so both sides of it have steep embankments, making it impossible to cross without some means of bridging it. In the feudal days the Forbidden City was heavily guarded. In case any one should venture to cross the moat, guards in watchtowers would shoot arrows, and soldiers would come out to arrest him.

Fourteen Ming emperors (Zhu Yuanzhang and Zhu Yunwen reigned from Nanjing) and ten Qing emperors lived in those splendid palaces, spanning a period of 491 years. Some of them were great men who made lasting contributions to the country and the people, but some were fatuous and self-indulgent rulers who lived lives of debauchery. As time passes, people's values change. It is necessary, I think, to re-examine these historical figures' merits and demerits, and give them appropriate appraisals.

After your visit to the Forbidden City, I suggest you go up to the Ten Thousand Spring Pavilion (Wanchunting) on top of Coal Hill (Jingshan) just to the north and get a bird's-eye view of the billowing roofs of the myriad palace buildings. There you will sense its grandeur, mystery and boundless charm. In the sunshine the red walls (red is a sign of happiness and auspiciousness) and yellow glazed roofs (yellow is a royal color) shimmer brightly. In between these buildings are green gardens with pavilions and grotesque rock formations. The vast squares, the exquisitely built watchtowers, the glimmering moat ... all show the grandeur of an ancient imperial palace. Indeed a splendid sight!

2. The Construction of the Forbidden City

Zhu Yuanzhang, founder of the Ming Dynasty, made Jinling (present-day Nanjing) his capital and bestowed upon his fourth son, Zhu Di, the title of Prince Yan and sent him to live in Beiping Prefecture. After Zhu Yuanzhang's death, his fourth grandson, Zhu Yunwen succeeded to the throne. In June 1402 Zhu Di rebelled, seized his nephew's throne and made himself emperor. The name of his reign period was Yongle. In early 1403, the first year of Yongle, he promoted Beiping Prefecture to Beijing City. Then he moved several hundred thousand people there from Nanjing, and Shanxi and Zhejiang provinces in five waves, so as to make the city stronger and bigger.

In 1406 Emperor Zhu Di came to Beijing himself to supervise the building of the Imperial Palace. The construction was completed in 1413. Unfortunately, before long, it first caught fire and later was hit by an earthquake. The new palace was almost entirely destroyed. It was then rebuilt in 1416, and completed in 1420. In 1421 Zhu Di moved his court to Beijing, which then became the capital.

Later, the Imperial Palace was renovated and enlarged by various emperors and became even more magnificent.

3. The Layout of the Forbidden City

Construction of the Forbidden City followed the principle of "offices in front, living quarters at the back; ancestors on the left and gods on the right." The emperor held court with his ministers in the halls in the front part of the Palace. The back part was the living quarters of the emperor, empress, consorts and so on. Sacrificial ceremonies to the imperial ancestors were held in the Ancestral Temple (Taimiao) on the left side, which has now been converted into the Workers' Palace of Culture. On its right lies the area containing the Altars of Land and Grain, which is now called Zhongshan Park. Coal Hill to the north of the Forbidden City is like a screen protecting the Imperial Palace from that direction.

Lying in the center of Beijing, the Forbidden City was built on a north-south axis, and the throne is located right on the axis. This symbolized that the emperor was the center of the universe. It also meant that all land under Heaven belonged to the emperor, and all people under Heaven were the emperor's subjects.

4. Why Is It Called the Forbidden City?

Why is this imperial palace called the Forbidden City?

Chinese emperors all styled themselves the "Son of Heaven." That is to say, the emperor was the supreme ruler under Heaven. Therefore, his palace was off-limits to commoners. People were not allowed to approach it. So it was commonly called the Forbidden City.

5. Manpower for the Construction

During the construction craftsmen and laborers were time and again recruited throughout China. Each time, some 100,000 craftsmen and a million laborers were mobilized for the project. The total of the manpower and building materials used for the construction is incalculable.

Take timber for example. Huge trees felled in the forests of Sichuan, Guizhou, Guangxi, Hunan and Yunnan had to be transported by water all the way to Beijing because they were too heavy to carry by any other means.

White marble was obtained from Fangshan County, on the

outskirts of Beijing, colored stones from Jixian County in Hebei Province and granite from Quyang County, also in Hebei. In bitterly cold winters roads leading to Beijing were splashed with water so that sleds could drag the chunks of rock along the ice. To provide water for the purpose, wells were dug along the way, one every 500 m. In summer logs were used to roll the rocks, one large rock often requiring several hundred people to move it.

Wall bricks came from Linqing in Shandong Province, and square floor bricks were transported to Beijing all the way from Suzhou in Jiangsu Province. These high-quality floor bricks would give out a metallic sound when tapped and were known as "golden bricks." Glazed tiles were produced in two major kilns. First, they were made exclusively in the Liulichang (Glazed-Tile Factory) in Beijing. Later, another kiln in Liuliqucun (Glazed-Tile Canal Village) in Mentougou in the suburbs of Beijing, began to fire glazed tiles for the Palace too.

6. Sightseeing Routes in the Forbidden City

The Forbidden City is divided into two parts, namely, the Outer Palace and the Inner Palace.

The Outer Palace was where imperial ceremonies were held, and where the emperor and his ministers carried out their official duties. It includes the Gate of Heavenly Peace (Tiananmen), Meridian Gate (Wumen), Hall of Supreme Harmony (Taihedian), Hall of Central Harmony (Zhonghedian), Hall of Preserving Harmony (Baohedian) and buildings along the central axis. The main structures are the three halls, known as the Three Great Halls. To the east of the three halls lies the Hall of Literary Flowers (Wenhuadian); to the west, the Hall of Military Strength (Wuyingdian).

The Inner Palace consists of the Palace of Heavenly Purity (Qianqinggong), Hall of Celestial and Terrestrial Union (Jiaotaidian), Palace of Earthly Tranquility (Kunninggong) and Imperial Garden, all on the central axis, and six palaces beside them. It served as the living quarters of the imperial household throughout the Ming and Qing dynasties.

There are four sightseeing routes open to the public at present.

The Middle Route takes in the Meridian Gate, the Hall of Supreme Harmony, Hall of Central Harmony, Hall of Preserving Harmony, Palace of Heavenly Purity, Hall of Celestial and Terrestrial Union, Palace of Earthly Tranquility, Imperial Garden and Gate of Divine Might (Shenwumen).

The Western Route takes in the Six Western Palaces [Palace for Gathering Elegance (Chuxiugong), Hall of Manifest Harmony (Tihedian), Palace of Modest Ladies (Yikungong), Palace of Eternal Spring (Changchungong), Hall of Manifest Origin (Tiyuandian) and Hall of the Supreme Ultimate (Taijidian)], and Hall of Mental Cultivation.

The Eastern Route takes in the main structures including the Six Eastern Palaces [Palace of Great Benevolence (Jingrengong), Palace of Celestial Favor (Chengqiangong), Palace of Eternal Harmony (Yonghegong), Palace of Quintessence (Zhongcuigong), Palace of Great Brilliance (Jingyanggong) and Hall to Usher in Happiness (Yanxigong)], and the Palace of Abstinence (Zhaigong).

The Outer Eastern Route (further east than the Eastern Route) mainly includes the Hall for Ancestral Worship (Fengxiandian), Nine Dragon Screen (Jiulongbi), Hall of Imperial Supremacy (Huangjidian), Palace of Tranquil Longevity (Ningshougong), Pavilion of Cheerful Melodies (Changyinge), Hall of Joyful Longevity (Leshoutang) and Qianlong Garden.

The Forbidden City is accessible both from the south (Wumen) and the north (Shenwumen).

Apart from these buildings erected some 570 years ago, one may also view cultural relics and treasures from the collection in the Imperial Palace.

1. Cultural Relics: Cultural relics are mostly exhibited along the Middle Route and the Western Route. Many buildings both in the Outer Palace and Inner Palace are furnished as they used to be.

2. Treasures: Along the Eastern Route there are exhibitions of bronzes, ceramics, and arts and crafts of the Ming and Qing dynasties. The Exhibition of Fine Arts and Exhibition of Treasures

are on the Outer Eastern Route. If you have plenty of time you may visit all these exhibitions, but if your time is limited take the Middle Route first, then the Western Route or the Eastern Route.

Chapter Two
The Main Structures in the Forbidden City

1. The Meridian Gate—Main Entrance to the Forbidden City

The Meridian Gate (Wumen), the main entrance to the Forbidden City, is a huge structure built in the shape of the letter "U". Of all the four entrances to the Forbidden City it is the most magnificent. The red wall alone is 13 m high. On top of the central wall there is a large rostrum with double-eaved roof. It is altogether 37.95 m from the ground to the top of the roof. On both corners of the Wumen facade there are towers, and at each end of the side walls there is a square-shaped pavilion. Therefore, there are five structures on top of the wall, giving rise to Wumen's informal name of Five-Phoenix Tower (Wufenglou).

A throne was placed on the rostrum, flanked by a Drum Tower and a Bell Tower. Whenever the emperor went out to perform sacrificial rites at the city's altars the bell would ring. When the emperor went to the Ancestral Temple the drum would be beaten. When an important imperial ceremony was held, both the bell and drum would sound; they could be heard five km away.

On the occasion of the Lantern Festival, which falls on the 15th day of the first lunar month, the emperor would hold a grand feast to entertain his civil officials and military officers. On the occasion, colorful lanterns would be hung on the rostrum. The emperor and his subordinates would enjoy themselves by viewing the lanterns and composing poems. It was also here that the emperor held parties and handed out some delicacies such as spring cake at *lichun* (the Beginning of Spring), glutinous cakes at the Dragon Boat Festival (the 5th day of the 5th lunar month), steamed rice cakes at the Double Ninth Festival (the 9th day of the 9th lunar month), etc.

On the first day of the 10th lunar month a ceremony to issue the next year's lunar calendar was held here too.

When a general returned triumphantly from a battle the emperor would hold a ceremony here to celebrate the victory. Here too, the general would symbolically turn over his captives to the emperor.

The Meridian Gate actually has five gateways; three on its facade and two on the sides. The one in the center was normally used by the emperor only. The empress was allowed to enter the Palace through this main gate only on the occasion of her wedding. The other people who were given the honor of going through this gate were the *Zhuangyuan* (winner of the first place in the imperial examination of the highest level), the *Tanhua* (winner of the second place) and the *Bangyan* (winner of the third place).

It was also at the Meridian Gate that officials who had incurred the emperor's disfavor were flogged with cudgels on their buttocks. During the Ming Dynasty, Emperor Jiajing wanted to go to the Yangtze River Valley to select beauties to be his concubines. When some officials tried to dissuade him the enraged emperor had 134 of them flogged. Seventeen were beaten to death. This punishment was carried out by *jinyiwei* (the Embroidered-Uniform) guards (the secret police of the Ming Dynasty). The one to be punished would have to wear prison garb and be put into a sack, his hands tied with rope. The guards did the flogging by turns. When one guard had whacked him five times, he would be replaced by another. Over 100 guards stood around and echoed the yell "Start flogging." No wonder many died of such torture.

Because of worsening political corruption, the reign of Emperor Jiajing (1521-1567) marked the beginning of the decline of the Ming Dynasty.

2. Inner Golden Stream—A Splendid Man-Made River

When you go through the Meridian Gate you come to a

man-made river shaped to resemble a Tartar bow, its water flowing from west to east. This is the Inner Golden Stream. It is spanned by five stone bridges with artistically carved marble balustrades. The water comes from the moat in the northwest and flows slowly towards the south, entering the moat again in the southeast. Sometimes it flows in the open and can be seen and sometimes it flows underground. The five bridges were built over the widest part of the Inner Golden Stream.

The central bridge over the Inner Golden Stream is called the Imperial Bridge, for only the emperor was allowed to use it. Its balustrades are elaborately carved with a motif of dragons and clouds. The two bridges right beside it were used by other members of the imperial household. So they were named Nobles' Bridges. The two further off were for officials above the third grade. Therefore, they were known as High-Ranking Officials' Bridges. Their balustrades are carved with a lotus motif.

3. The Gate of Supreme Harmony—Where the Emperor Discharged His Official Duties

Beyond the Meridian Gate there stands the Gate of Supreme Harmony (Taihemen). In front of this gate there is a square measuring 26,000 sq m. This gate is the highest and largest archway in the Forbidden City. It is nine bays wide and four bays deep, taking up an area of 1,300 sq m.

During the Ming Dynasty a throne was placed in the center of this structure. It was here that the emperor held conferences with his ministers. At dawn the Gate of Supreme Harmony was brightly lit with lanterns, and officials and military officers gathered here waiting for the emperor to arrive, when he would be greeted by kowtows. The emperor would first deal with memorandums submitted by his ministers. This shows that the rulers of the early Ming were diligent administrators, but by the reign of Emperor Wanli (1572-1620) the emperor no longer held early morning discussions with his ministers. Naturally, as state affairs were neglected, politics grew more and more corrupt.

During the Qing Dynasty the imperial court was held in the Palace of Heavenly Purity in the Inner Palace. The Gate of Supreme Harmony was where the emperor received presents, held celebration ceremonies and gave banquets.

Whenever the emperor went out on inspections he would first ride in a sedan-chair and then change to a carriage at the Gate of Supreme Harmony. It was also here that the emperor received foreign envoys and other foreign dignitaries.

4. The Hall of Supreme Harmony—Where Grand Imperial Ceremonies Were Held

The Hall of Supreme Harmony (Taihedian), also known as the Hall of the Golden Throne (Jinluandian), is the largest structure in the Forbidden City. The hall itself is 26.92 m high. If its base is included it is 35.05 m high. It is 11 bays wide and five bays deep, occupying a floor area of 2,377 sq m. Since it was used by the emperor its size, design, arrangement and furniture were most elaborately planned and were the most luxurious of their day. Usually, on the eave extensions of roof corners there were three, five, seven or, at most, nine (all odd numbers) decorative figurines of immortals and mythical beasts. But an exception was made for the Hall of Supreme Harmony—there are ten (see Fig. 1). This is the only exception in the whole country. On each end of its main roof ridge there is a large dragon, 3.4 m high and 4,300 kg in weight. On the base wall there are 1,142 rain spouts made of marble in the shape of dragon heads. On the southeast corner of the stairway there is a sundial, and on the southwest, there is a standard measuring container. Both devices indicated the power of the emperor, for they meant that he was the master of both time and space. Apart from these, on display are also a bronze tortoise and a bronze crane, both signs of longevity. In those days, they indicated a wish for long life for the imperial power.

As soon as you enter the Hall of Supreme Harmony you will see a large chair decorated with gilded entwined dragons. It is set on a platform up a flight of seven steps. This is the throne. It is

The gargoyles on the roof ridge of the Hall of Supreme Harmony, from the right: immortal, dragon, phoenix, lion, sea horse, heavenly steed, *ya* fish, *suanni*, *xiezhi*, the Dipper ox and *xingshi*. All these are mythical beasts.

flanked by two gilded *luduan*, one on each side. The *luduan* is said to be a four-legged mythical beast with one horn on its head. It could cover 9,000 km in a day and understand all kinds of languages. If the emperor was a wise and just one they would come with books to serve him. To each side of the throne are three giant columns decorated with golden dragons. They are more than ten m in height and are wider than two armspans. There are altogether 72 pillars inside and outside the hall. Six giant columns around the throne are gilded and, therefore, golden in color, while all the rest are painted vermilion. The dragons entwining the three eastern columns all look west, while the dragons entwining the three western columns all look east.

The Hall of Supreme Harmony is a world of dragons. Dragons frolic on the screen behind the throne, as well as entwining columns. Directly above the throne is an exquisitely carved interior cupola filled with a coiled dragon from whose mouth hangs a mirrored sphere on a chain. It has been calculated that there are altogether 13,844 dragons in this hall alone.

Grandiose ceremonies would be held here on occasions such as an emperor's ascension to the throne, wedding and bestowing the title of empress on his bride, as well as the lunar New Year, the Winter Solstice and the emperor's birthday, when all officials and military officers would pay homage to the emperor. It was also here that a ceremony was held when a general was dispatched on an expedition during the Qing Dynasty. The general would bow beforethe imperial flag and then receive a cup of wine from the emperor. When a general returned in triumph the emperor would give him and his men a big banquet and take back the "Seal of the Commander." On such an occasion, the route from the Hall of Supreme Harmony to the Gate of Heavenly Peace (Tiananmen) would be lined with banners. An orchestra would be called in to play music on the platform outside the hall. When the emperor took his seat golden bells and jade chimes sounded, and all officials and military officers knelt down on the platform in the square. Incense inside the bronze tortoise and crane burned, emitting plumes of smoke all around the hall. After the ceremony a feast was given. Those who were allowed to attend the feast inside the hall were princes, and officials of the first and second grades. Hereditary officials above the second grade could dine on the red stairway. Officials below the third grade and foreign envoys all sat in the 16 blue tents on the east and west sides of the square. Each high-ranking official had a two-foot-high table placed before him; the others shared tables, usually two or three to one table. Without exception, everyone had to sit on the floor. At one large banquet during the early Qing Dynasty 210 tables were laid. More than 100 sheep and 100 bottles of liquor were consumed. Such feasts were very formal and ceremonious, involving much ceremony and kowtowing. They were probably not very pleasant occasions.

The ceremony for an emperor's ascension to the throne was most pompous. During the Ming and Qing dynasties 24 emperors were enthroned. When Aisin-Gioro Pu Yi, the last emperor of the Qing Dynasty, came to the throne he was only three years old. His father, Regent Zaifeng, had to carry him wailing to the throne. His father said to him: "Stop! Don't cry! It'll soon be over." Pu Yi's reign lasted for only three years and the Qing Dynasty came to an end.

Later, some people put the blame on the regent for having uttered inauspicious words.

5. The Hall of Central Harmony—Where the Emperor Rested Before Grand Ceremonies

The Hall of Central Harmony (Zhonghedian) is a square structure built like a pavilion. Each side is five bays long, measuring 24.15 m. It is located between the Hall of Supreme Harmony and the Hall of Preserving Harmony. These three halls, known as the Three Great Halls, are the center of the Forbidden City. Of the three halls, the Hall of Central Harmony is the smallest. A bird's-eye view shows that such an architectural arrangement avoids monotony. This indicates that the ancient architects had a high level of expertise.

On the roof there is a gilded pinnacle which gleams brightly in the sunshine. Compared with the Hall of Supreme Harmony, this hall is simply furnished. However, in its center there is also a throne.

On the occasion of the New Year, Winter Solstice and the emperor's birthday, grand ceremonies would be held in the Hall of Supreme Harmony. On his way to the hall the emperor would take a rest in the Hall of Central Harmony. When everything was ready he would go to the Hall of Supreme Harmony to receive homage.

The emperor usually took a sedan-chair to the Three Great Halls from the Inner Palace. There are two sedan-chairs on display in the Hall of Central Harmony—one black, one colorfully decorated. They both have motifs of dragons and clouds. They needed eight bearers, and others even needed 16 bearers.

Every spring the emperor would go to the Altar of the God of Agriculture (Xiannongtan) in southern Beijing to plow land and sow seeds himself. This marked the beginning of spring plowing for the whole country. Before this, the emperor would go to the Hall of Central Harmony to prepare the elegiac address used for the ceremony and to see if the farm tools and seeds were ready. The following day, followed by a contingent of officials and guards, he went to the Altar of the God of Agriculture to hold the ceremony.

Amidst the sounds of drums and gongs the emperor began to plow the land and sow seeds. He plowed and sowed four furrows and then announced the beginning of spring plowing.

The imperial family tree of the Qing Dynasty was compiled once every ten years. When the compilation was finished it would be sent to the emperor to be examined. This was done in the Hall of Central Harmony.

6. The Hall of Preserving Harmony—Where the Highest-Level Civil Service Examination Was Held

The Hall of Preserving Harmony (Baohedian) is nine bays (49.68 m) wide and five bays (24.97 m) deep. Its interior appears rather large because there are few pillars in it.

A special feature of this hall is a colossal rock, known as the Rock of Dragons on Clouds, in the rear. It is 16.57 m long, 3.07 m wide and 1.7 m thick, and it weighs 250 tons. Carved on the rock are nine dragons frolicking amidst clouds. They are all very lifelike and vivid. This rock was found in Fangshan, in the western suburbs of Beijing. According to historical records, in bitterly cold winter people fetched water from wells, one at every 50-m interval, and splashed it over the surface of the 50-km-long road. When the water was frozen hard the rock was pushed and drawn by more than 20,000 men and 1,000 mules and horses. It took them 28 days to reach the Forbidden City.

In 1789 (the 54th year of the reign of Emperor Qianlong of the Qing Dynasty) the venue of the highest level of the imperial civil service examination was moved from the Hall of Supreme Harmony to this hall. Only those who had passed the imperial examinations at the levels of county, prefecture and province were qualified to sit for this examination. The text for the examination had to be approved by the emperor himself. All the completed papers were examined by ministers designated by the emperor, and the choices of the top-ten successful candidates were also approved by the emperor. The top three were regarded as being in the first grade. The one who won the first place was called *Zhuangyuan*, the second

Bangyan and the third *Tanhua*. They would then be appointed high-ranking officials by the emperor. Those in the categories of the second and third grades were named *Jinshi*, and they would later be appointed officials by the emperor after a further test. This was how the emperor selected his high-ranking officials.

The Hall of Preserving Harmony and its wing chambers have now been converted into an art exhibition hall, in which more than 1,600 pieces of artistic works, including ceramics, bronzes, jades, paintings and calligraphy, covering over 6,000 years from primitive society to the Qing Dynasty are on display.

7. The Gate of Heavenly Purity—Entrance to the Quarters of the Imperial Household

Right behind the Hall of Preserving Harmony there is a square which is 200 m long and 50 m wide. This narrow stretch of land separated the Outer Palace from the Inner Palace. To the north of this square is the Gate of Heavenly Purity (Qianqingmen), the entrance to the living quarters of the imperial household. The Zhou Dynasty (11 century B.C.-476 B.C.) stipulated that the palace of an emperor should have five formal entrances. Abiding by this rule, the Ming and Qing emperors all had five formal entrances, namely, the Gate of Heavenly Peace, the Gate of Correct Demeanor, the Meridian Gate, the Gate of Supreme Harmony and the Gate of Heavenly Purity. In front of this gate there squat two gilded copper lions guarding it. On each side of the gate there are four large gilded copper vats. Some Qing emperors also held court here. Ministers and other officials would gather here at dawn waiting for the emperor to come. There was a temporary throne, and the emperor would sit here to listen to memorandums presented to him by the kneeling ministers in the order of those in charge of the boards of Revenue, Rites, War, Works and Civil Office. Decisions would be made by the emperor. Emperor Kangxi (who ruled for 61 years from 1662 to 1723) was the most diligent of the Qing emperors. Many important decisions were made by him at the Gate of Heavenly Purity.

As the main entrance to the living quarters, the Gate of Heavenly Purity was heavily guarded. There were two officers of the eighth grade in charge of security. But when the emperor held court there were a lot more guards and officers guarding the place. It was stipulated that during these sessions imperial family members below the rank of prince and duke, officials above the third grade and military officers above the second grade and those serving in the Inner Palace were not allowed to enter the Longzong Gate to the west of Qianqingmen or the Jingyun Gate to the east if they had no memorandums to present. The people in the entourages of the officials had to stay 20 m away from these two gates. Though guarded like this, the square was not always impenetrable. On the 15th day of the ninth lunar month in the 18th year of the reign of Emperor Jiaqing (1813), peasants in the suburbs of Beijing started an uprising and, aided by some eunuchs, attacked the Imperial Palace. They had entered the city under the cover of darkness the previous night and tried to enter the Palace from two sides. One group attacked the Western Flowery Gate (Xihuamen) and soon reached the Longzong Gate. The other contingent had a skirmish with some coal carriers at the Eastern Flowery Gate (Donghuamen), and the guards managed to shut the gate against them. The Longzong Gate too was finally barred to the insurgents after a bitter struggle.

8. The Palace of Heavenly Purity—Living Quarters of the Emperor

Right behind the Gate of Heavenly Purity there stands a building named the Palace of Heavenly Purity (Qianqinggong), which is nine bays wide and five bays deep. This is the largest and probably most important structure in the Inner Palace. It has a double-eaved roof and annex buildings around it. On each extended roof corner there are nine zoomorphic figurines. All the Ming emperors lived in this palace. *Qian* means Heaven and *qing* means clean. This meant that the imperial rule was flawless and stable. To the east is the Sun Gate (Rijingmen), and to the west, the Moon

Gate (Yuehuamen). Further east are the Six Eastern Palaces, and further west, the Six Western Palaces, symbolizing the 12 major stars in the sky. The clusters of buildings behind the Palace of Heavenly Purity were regarded as a galaxy of stars. This arrangement indicated that the Palace of Heavenly Purity, or Heaven, was the center of the universe, and the emperor, the son of Heaven, was the absolute ruler under Heaven.

In the Palace of Heavenly Purity there were nine bedrooms, all heated by heating pipes beneath the floor. Each room had two floors, and all the rooms were linked by stairs or corridors. In each room there were three beds, so in total there were 27 beds. Nobody knew which bed the emperor would sleep in at night, except his close eunuchs. This was a security measure, but the Palace of Heavenly Purity was not always peaceful despite those precautions. Once 16 palace maids headed by Yang Jinying tried to kill Emperor Jiajing, in an accident known as the "Renyin Coup." Several other attempts to assassinate emperors took place in this place.

On the 18th day of the third lunar month of the 17th year of the reign of Emperor Chongzhen (1644), Li Zicheng and his peasant army invaded Beijing. The emperor called his ministers to the Palace of Heavenly Purity to discuss the situation. That night, as the noise of the peasant army ransacking the city was heard, the emperor disguised himself as a eunuch and fled from the Forbidden City on horseback to the mansion of Zhu Chunchen, one of his high-ranking officials. But Zhu's guards refused to open the gate. The emperor had to return to the Palace of Heavenly Purity. He ordered his men to beat the drum and sound the bell to call his ministers to an emergency meeting. But not a single one turned up at this critical moment. The emperor, together with his favorite eunuch, then hurried to Coal Hill, where he hanged himself. His eunuch also killed himself. The Ming Dynasty thus came to an end. However, some of the Ming imperial family set up the Southern Ming Dynasty in the south, which lasted 18 years. It was finally wiped out by Qing forces.

The Palace of Heavenly Purity was renovated after the Qing

Dynasty set up its capital in Beijing. It was used as living quarters by emperors Shunzhi and Kangxi. It was here that they held court, received foreign envoys and studied. When Yongzheng became emperor he moved his quarters to the Hall of Mental Cultivation (Yangxindian). He used this hall to hold ceremonies, discuss stateaffairs with his ministers and receive foreign emissaries. On the occasions of the Spring Festival, Lantern Festival, Dragon Boat Festival, Mid-Autumn Festival, Winter Solstice and the emperor's birthday, banquets were given for members of the imperial household in the Palace of Heavenly Purity. There were two grand banquets held here in honor of elderly men: On the Spring Festival of year 1722, more than 1,000 old men were invited, and in 1786 another banquet was held to entertain some 3,000 old men.

The way of choosing a successor to the throne during the Qing Dynasty was peculiar. Behind a horizontal plaque on which the words "Justice and Brightness" were written hung in this hall there was a casket. In the casket was a piece of silk on which the name of his successor was written by the emperor. A duplicate copy was in the possession of the emperor himself. Only when he died were ministers allowed to open the casket and announce the name of the new emperor in public. Emperors Qianlong, Jiaqing, Daoguang and Xianfeng were all chosen in this way.

The east wing chamber of the Palace of Heavenly Purity has been turned into an exhibition hall of Qing-era decrees, documents and so on. One can view emperors' seals, musical instruments once used in the Qing court, garments worn by emperors and empresses and some weapons the imperial guards used.

9. The Hall of Celestial and Terrestrial Union

The Hall of Celestial and Terrestrial Union (Jiaotaidian) is located between the Palace of Heavenly Purity and the Palace of Earthly Tranquility (Kunninggong). In Chinese, *qian* means Heaven and *kun* means earth. Therefore, the Hall of Celestial and Terrestrial Union is a place where Heaven and earth are supposed to merge. The name also indicates that everything is peaceful and harmonious.

Built in the shape of a square, each side as long as three bays, it is a single-roof structure with a gilded bronze spherical pinnacle. Though similar to the Hall of Preserving Harmony in architectural style, this hall is smaller. This was where the emperors received homage paid by ministers and others. On her birthday the emperor's consorts and concubines, and wives of regents and princes would come here to pay their respects to the empress. On the occasions of the Winter Solstice and the Spring Festival people also came here to pay their respect to the empress.

Since the 11th year of the reign of Emperor Qianlong (1746) the 25 imperial seals of the emperor were kept here. The imperial seals were signs of power. Each seal had its special purpose. They were used for political affairs, military affairs, judicial affairs, affairs concerning nationalities, the imperial household, diplomacy, education, etc. All these seals were carefully guarded, and could only be used at the order of the emperor.

The 5.8-m high clock in this hall was made by craftsmen of the Palace in 1798. It still works today and its chime is as clear and resonant as ever.

10. The Palace of Earthly Tranquility—Nuptial Chamber of the Emperor and Empress

The Palace of Earthly Tranquility (Kunninggong), the last of the Three Great Palaces, was where empresses lived during the Ming Dynasty. But during the Qing period it served only as the nuptial chamber of the emperor and empress, and they only spent three days here. The empress would then move to another dwelling place.

Twenty-two m high, the palace is nine bays wide and five bays deep. Like the Palace of Heavenly Purity, it is also a structure with a double-eaved roof and side buildings. However, it is smaller.

The Qing emperors and empresses were all rather superstitious. Following the Manchu custom, they turned the four rooms at the western end of the Palace of Earthly Tranquility into an altar for worshipping the deities. Sacrifices were offered twice a day, one in the morning, the other in the evening. Grand ceremonies would be held here on Spring Festival, and in spring and autumn, which both the emperor and empress would attend. On such occasions, cakes would be steamed and meat cooked. After the ceremony everybody, including the emperor, would have a share of the cakes and meat. For the daily sacrificial rites, four pigs were slaughtered, but for special ceremonies 39 pigs were slaughtered at a time. Since there was plenty of meat available in the Palace, the eunuchs were not above stealing some and selling it in the city.

The two rooms in the east of this palace once served as the nuptial quarters for the emperor and empress. Their interior walls were painted red, and red palace lanterns with the Chinese character meaning "double happiness" on them were hung high there. The screen in front was also pasted with the word meaning "happiness." It was an auspicious sign, for whenever the emperor or empress opened the door, he or she would first see that character. The bed canopy was called the "Hundred Children Canopy." The quilts were embroidered with the figures of 100 children, hence the name "Hundred Children Quilts." All this was to wish the emperor and empress a lot of children and long lives full of happiness.

11. The Imperial Garden—Leisure Park of the Imperial Household

Behind the Palace of Earthly Tranquility is the Imperial Garden, where members of the imperial household often came to enjoy their leisure time.

Some 12,000 sq m in extent, the Imperial Garden has 20 structures, all in different architectural styles, with the Hall of Imperial Peace (Qinandian) as its center. Due to all the buildings and trees, one can not have a panoramic view of the whole garden at one glance. Therefore, there are constant delights and surprises as you walk around it. This garden teems with ancient pine and cypress trees, flowers, grotesque rock formations and so on. It is typical of an imperial garden.

The Hall of Imperial Peace, lying on the north-south axis, is located in the northernmost part of the Forbidden City. In ancient

Chinese architecture, north was associated with water. A statue of Zhenwu, the God of Water in the Daoist legends was housed in the hall. On the occasions of the Beginning of Spring, Summer, Autumn and Winter the emperor came here to pay homage to God of Water and entreated him to protect the people from floods.

In the northeast of the garden there stands a 14-m-high rock formation known as the Hill of Splendor (Duixiushan). In front of it there are a pair of stone-carved dragon heads. Water spouted out of their mouths as high as 10 m in the air and tiny water beads formed in mid-air glittering in the sunshine. A winding path leads to the Pavilion of the Imperial Scene (Yujingting) on the top of the hill. On the Double Ninth Festival (ninth day of the ninth lunar month) the emperor, accompanied by his empress and concubines, would climb to the top of this hill, from where they could see all the halls and palaces in the Forbidden City. If it was a fine day they could even see the Western Hills in the distance.

In the southeast of the garden there is the Chamber of Crimson Snow (Jiangxuexuan). Opposite, i.e. in the southwest, lies the Chamber of Character Cultivation (Yangxingzhai), a library built in the style of a pavilion.

The winding paths in this garden are all paved with tiny, colorful stones. On the paths, there are more than 900 mosaics all told. They are well worth studying.

On the seventh day of the seventh lunar month, the emperor and empress would come here to burn joss-sticks to two stars—the Cowherd (Altair) and the Weaving Girl (Vega), two legendary figures who were said to have fallen in love and to meet once a year on this day in the Milky Way. At the Mid-Autumn Festival, which falls on the 15th day of the eighth lunar month, they came to the garden to enjoy the full moon.

In the garden there are a dozen *lianli* ("clinging to each other") trees, which have all been cultivated from pine and cypress trees. There is a story about *lianli* trees. During the Warring States Period (475-221 B.C.) King Kang coveted the beautiful wife of Han Ping. So he sent Han away to work on some fortifications. But when the work was completed the king had him killed and then coerced Han's wife to marry him. She agreed on condition that a grand funeral be held for her husband. The king consented, but at the funeral the wife killed herself by throwing herself into the grave. King Kang buried them together. The following year two trees grew out of the grave with their upper branches entwined around one another—hence the name *lianli*. They were regarded as a sign of everlasting love.

There was once an attempt to assassinate an emperor here that nearly succeeded. On April 11, 1803, on his way to his quarters, Emperor Jiaqing encountered an armed stranger who chased him to the Shunzhen Gate, the northern gate of the Imperial Garden. Not a single one of more than 100 guards attempted to help the emperor, but the man was finally overcome and arrested by attendant ministers and their bodyguards. The would-be assassin was put to death "by a thousand cuts" upon the order of the emperor.

12. The Six Western Palaces—Living Quarters of the Imperial Household

The Six Western Palaces, situated to the west of the Three Great Palaces, were the living quarters of the emperor, the empress and the imperial concubines.

The Six Western Palaces refer to the Palace for Gathering Elegance, Hall of Manifest Harmony, Palace of Modest Ladies, Palace of Eternal Spring, Hall of Manifest Origin and Hall of the Supreme Ultimate, each of which has its own courtyard. Dotted in these courtyards are all kinds of flowers and trees. Under colorfully painted and elaborately carved beams and rafters, life was colorful and eventful here.

The Palace for Gathering Elegance was the dwelling place of Empress Dowager Cixi from the time she entered the Forbidden City and was bestowed the title of Consort Orchid. She gave birth to one son by Emperor Xianfeng. This son later became Emperor Tongzhi. On the occasion of her 50th birthday this palace was renovated. All the beams and rafters were painted with flowers, birds, fish, insects, landscapes and human figures, which Cixi loved. Bronze dragons and deer were moved in as decorations, and the walls of the corridor were carved with ministers' eulogies in praise of her. Today, it remains as it looked at that very time. The miniature flowers made of jadeite, jade and precious stones on the table, srolls made of ivory hanging on the wall, palace lanterns suspended from the ceiling and the exquisitely-made dressing table all show the extravagance of the imperial house.

The Hall of Manifest Harmony, lying to the south of the Palace for Gathering Elegance, was where Empress Dowager Cixi dined. According to historical records, she had two formal meals and two snacks a day. There were some 450 people employed for this purpose alone. At each meal there were more than 100 meat and vegetable dishes and scores of staple food items. But all this was only for show, because she only touched a few of them.

It was here that the empress dowager once put on a farce of selecting an empress for Emperor Guangxu. There were five candidates for the final. They were a daughter of an army commander-in-chief, two daughters of the governor of Jiangxi and two daughters of a deputy minister of the Ministry of Rites. On a table there were a jade *ruyi* (S-shaped ornamental object, a symbol of good luck) and two red embroidered purses. The one chosen for the empress by the emperor would be given the *ruyi*; the ones chosen for a concubine, the purses. Guangxu chose one of the governor's daughters for his empress. But just as he was about to offer the jade *ruyi* to her, Cixi cried out hastily: "Emperor!" Having taken her hint, he gave the *ruyi* to the daughter of the army commander-in-chief. This girl was later to become Empress Longyu. She was by no means good-looking, and even a few years senior to the emperor. But she was a niece of Cixi's. Guangxu had no alternative but to subject himself to this political arrangement. Fearing that the two daughters of the governor might be chosen by the emperor as concubines who might one day become his favorites, Cixi made the emperor take the daughters of the deputy minister as his concubines. The two girls were later to become Consort Jin and Consort Zhen. So the supreme ruler's wedding was thus manipulated by Cixi, which resulted in tragedy later.

The Palace of Modest Ladies was the residence of the imperial concubines during both the Ming and Qing dynasties. When Cixi lived in the Palace for Gathering Elegance she often received morning greetings from imperial concubines here. On her 50th birthday ministers came here to extend their congratulations to her.

The Palace of Longevity also served as living quarters for the imperial concubines during these two dynasties. Its corridors are decorated with episodes from the classic novel *A Dream of Red Mansions*. The artists' brushstrokes indicate a high degree of artistic skill. Linking its courtyard with the back wall of the Hall of Manifest Origin is a stage for performances, known as the Stage of the Palace of Eternal Spring, where Cixi often came to watch performances.

The Hall of Mental Cultivation, standing to the west of the plaza of the Palace of Heavenly Purity, is made up of the Gate of Mental Cultivation, the Hall of Mental Cultivation and the Rear Hall in an independent courtyard. The floor area of these buildings is over 5,000 sq m. Apart from the Three Great Halls in the Outer Palace and the Three Great Palaces in the Inner Palace, this is the most striking structure in the Forbidden City. Since the Qing Emperor Yongzheng, eight Qing emperors used the Hall of Mental Cultivation as their quarters (All the Ming emperors and the Qing emperors Shunzhi and Kangxi lived in the Palace of Heavenly Purity). The halls in the center and the rear are connected; the emperor often worked, studied and received ministers in the central hall and lived in the rear hall. These buildings are surrounded by a corridor. Though not as magnificent as the Palace of Heavenly Purity, these living quarters are well composed, neat and comfortable. From the time of Emperor Yongzheng, they actually functioned as a center of government.

Since the emperor often held consultations with his ministers and received foreign emissaries here, there was a throne for him in the central hall. The western chamber was where the emperor read memorandums, wrote instructions and handled daily routine matters. Today, one can still see a list of local officials' names and a record of numbers of officials on its western wall. The western end of the chamber was called the "Home of Three Rarities," as it was here that the emperor housed three calligraphic masterpieces executed by the great Jin Dynasty (265-420) calligraphers Wang Xizhi (*Clearing up After Snow*), his son Wang Xianzhi (*Mid-Autumn*) and his nephew (*Boyuan*). The eastern chamber was once used by Cixi, who consulted ministers while shielded by a curtain.

One can go to the rear hall straight from the back of the central hall. The emperor had bedrooms in both the eastern and western wings of the rear hall. The furniture of those two bedrooms are on display there. To the east is the Tishun Chamber, which served as the bedroom for the emperor and empress when they were staying in the Hall of Mental Cultivation. The Yanxi Chamber and its annexes to the west were the residences of the imperial concubines, who waited to be called by the emperor to spend the night with him.

On the 20th of August, 1861, when Emperor Xianfeng died of illness, his only son, six-year old Zai Chun, (known as Emperor Tongzhi) succeeded to the throne. Before he died, Emperor Xianfeng had stipulated in his will that eight of his ministers should help the young emperor to rule the country. Zai Chun's mother, the 27-year old Cixi, was excluded, but this ambitious woman collaborated through her favorite eunuch An Dehai with the young emperor's sixth uncle Yi Xin to get rid of the regents. She had the eight ministers killed or sent into exile. From that time on, she and the late emperor's senior wife, known as the Eastern Dowager, began to attend to state affairs. This coup is known as the "Xinyou Coup."

When holding imperial court, the emperor sat on the throne while the two dowagers sat behind the throne, screened by a yellow silk curtain. They listened to memorandums, made decisions and issued decrees on behalf of the emperor, who was merely a puppet.

Since the Eastern Dowager was a weak woman by nature, Cixi became the real ruler.

According to custom, Emperor Tongzhi should have taken over the power when he reached the age of 14. However, his mother was unwilling to give up power, and it was only when the emperor was 18 and got married did the Empress Dowager announced on March 26, 1873 to give the ruling power back to the emperor. But from time to time she intervened in state affairs. Therefore, the mother and the son often clashed, in fact their conflicts grew daily. Tongzhi died at the age of 19, leaving no son. In order to maintain her position as, literally, the power behind the throne, Cixi maneuvered so that Tongzhi's younger cousin, her own younger sister's son, succeeded to the throne. This heir was four-year old Zai Tian, who later became Emperor Guangxu. This ensured that Cixi would continue to attend the imperial court behind the curtain. It was not until he reached the age of 19 that Cixi had to stop holding court behind the curtain. In the year 1898 Emperor Guangxu started a political reform, which greatly annoyed Cixi. She put the emperor under house arrest. So again she took over the imperial power and controlled the imperial court for the third time, until she died at the age of 74. So altogether, she ruled China for 48 years, which is regarded as one of the darkest and most corrupt periods in Chinese history.

Another Qing empress who held imperial court behind the curtain was Empress Longyu, wife of Emperor Guangxu. In November 1908 Empress Dowager Cixi and Emperor Guangxu died within two days of each other, and the three-year old Pu Yi assumed the throne. Empress Longyu began to hold court behind the curtain.

13. The Six Eastern Palaces—Treasure Stores of Art

Lying to the east of the Three Rear Palaces, the Six Eastern Palaces are the Palace of Great Benevolence, Palace of Celestial Favor, Palace of Eternal Harmony and Palace of Great Brilliance.

The Palace of Great Brilliance was the imperial library all

through the Qing Dynasty. It was where Emperor Kangxi and Emperor Qianlong read books. So Emperor Qianlong named it the "Learning Poetry Chamber" and wrote those three characters on a horizontal name plaque for the library. It has now been converted into the Exhibition Hall of Arts and Crafts of the Ming and Qing Dynasties. There is a rich variety of exhibits in this hall—lacquerware, and articles made of jade, glass, metal, bamboo, wood, ivory and so on. They show the high level of expertise craftsmen of that time had already acquired.

The Palace of Great Benevolence was the living quarters of the Ming and Qing imperial concubines. It has been converted, together with the Palace of Abstinence (Zhaigong) and the Chengsu Hall, into the Exhibition Hall of Bronzewares, displaying 500 pieces of bronze dating from as early as the Shang Dynasty (c. 16th—11th centuries B.C.) to the Warring States Period (475-221 B.C.). During the Shang and Zhou dynasties different bronze objects were used to differentiate social status. But after the Warring States Period bronze was mainly used for daily necessities and weaponry. The exhibits on display are mainly from the collection in the Forbidden City itself.

The Palace of Celestial Favor and the Palace of Eternal Harmony, once dwellings of imperial concubines, are now the Exhibition Hall of Ceramics. Some 700 pieces of ceramics manufactured during the period from the Neolithic era to the Qing Dynasty are on display. One can see how ceramics developed step by step in ancient China and find painted earthenware dating back 6,000 years, black pottery as thin as an eggshell made 5,000 years ago, famous tricolor glazed pottery of the Tang Dynasty (618-907) and some masterpieces from kilns of the Song Dynasty (960-1279). Besides, there is a rich variety of ceramics manufactured in Jingdezhen, the center of Chinese ceramics, since the Ming Dynasty. Exhibits here are also mainly selected from the Forbidden City's own collection.

The Palace of Quintessence was the living quarters of the Ming crown princes. It was used for housing imperial concubines during the Qing Dynasty. Now it has been converted into the Exhibition Hall of Stationery, displaying the "Four Treasures of the Study," namely, writing brushes, ink-sticks, *Xuan* paper and ink-slabs.

The Palace of Abstinence was where the emperor practiced abstinence from meat two nights before holding a ceremony to offer sacrifices to Heaven or Earth.

14. The Palace of Tranquil Longevity—A Little Forbidden City Within the Forbidden City

Further to the east of the Six Eastern Palaces, e.g., in the northeast of the Forbidden City, there is a cluster of buildings forming a composition of its own. This is the Palace of Tranquil Longevity (Ningshougong), also known as the Outer Eastern Palace. Rectangular in shape, it is a replica of the Three Great Halls and the Three Great Palaces of the Forbidden City. Its floor area is 46,000 sq m. This compound can also be divided into three parts —the eastern, central and western parts. The central part contains the Hall of Imperial Supremacy (Huangjidian), Palace of Tranquil Longevity, Hall for Cultivating the Character (Yangxingdian), Hall of Joyful Longevity (Leshoutang), Pavilion of Sustained Harmony (Yihexuan) and the Jingqi Chamber. The eastern part includes the Changyinge Stage, where the emperor and his family watched local operas, and the Yueshi Chamber. The western part is the Qianlong Garden. The whole place is surrounded by a tall, red perimeter wall. As a separate compound, and designed like the Forbidden City, the Palace of Tranquil Longevity is, therefore, also known as "a little Forbidden City within the Forbidden City."

The building of the Palace of Tranquil Longevity was Emperor Qianlong's idea. He resigned from the throne after being emperor for 60 years and then retired to a quiet place to meditate and pray. By ruling one year less, he showed his respect for his grandfather, Emperor Kangxi, who had ruled for 61 years. In the 37th year of his reign (1772) he began building the palace for this purpose. But he was already over 60 years old that year, and was not sure if his reign could last another 23 years. So the names he gave those buildings in the palace all had the connotation of longevity. Luckily, he lived for 89 years, the longest living of all the Qing emperors. In 1795, when he was 85, his reign lasted for exactly 60 years, and he abdicated in favor of his son, Emperor Jiaqing. However, under the pretext of "giving family instructions," he still kept hold of power. Sitting on his own throne in the Hall of Mental Cultivation, he attended to all state affairs. Emperor Jiaqing, already 36 years of age, was actually at his beck and call, never daring to make any decisions of his own. Emperor Qianlong never actually lived in the Palace of Tranquil Longevity, which he had prepared for his retirement; he only went there for a visit or two in his leisure time. Emperor Jiaqing bore a grudge against his father, though he dared not show it when he was alive. But as soon as his father died, the new emperor wasted no time in arresting and executing his father's favorite minister, He Shen.

When you enter the Palace of Tranquil Longevity, you first see a high glazed screen wall named the Nine-Dragon Wall. It is 29.4 m long and 3.5 m high. The nine large dragons, each having a pearl, frolic in a blue sea, vivid and lifelike. It is said that the middle part of the third white dragon was once damaged by fire. That meant the death penalty for the person involved. At this critical moment, a craftsman volunteered to replace the middle part with a new piece. He did the carving, replaced the original and painted it white overnight. So it passed as original. You may still find the traces of the repair on the third dragon from the left. There are two magic numbers, nine and five, connected with this screen wall. Apart from the nine dragons on the front wall, there are five on the top of it. The whole wall is made of 270 tiles. The number 270 can be divided by both five and nine. Nine is the highest odd number, while five is right in the middle of the odd numbers. In ancient China these two numbers indicated the supremacy of the emperor. The dragon in the center is painted yellow and purple. Yellow was a royal color.

This dragon is on the north-south axis, on which there also stand the Gate of Imperial Supremacy (Huangjimen), Gate of

Tranquil Longevity (Ningshoumen), Hall of Imperial Supremacy (Huangjidian) and Palace of Tranquil Longevity. It faces the imperial path leading to the Hall of Imperial Supremacy and a nine-dragon horizontal plaque under the hall's eaves. If you stand in front of the Hall of Imperial Supremacy and look southward through two opened palace gates, you can see this bright yellow dragon.

Having passed through the Gate of Imperial Supremacy and the Gate of Tranquil Longevity, one comes to the Hall of Imperial Supremacy, a double-eaved nine-bay-wide building. This was where the Imperial Regent, e.g., the father of the emperor, received ministers. The Palace of Tranquil Longevity, behind this hall, is a seven-bay structure. The rooms at its western end are connected to one another, and preparations for sacrificial rites were made there. When Emperor Qianlong transferred the imperial power to his son in 1796 he gave a grand banquet in honor of elderly men in the Hall of Imperial Supremacy and the Palace of Tranquil Longevity. Present at the banquet were 5,000 civil and military officials, nobles and commoners, all over 65 years old. Eight hundred tables were laid. Amidst the sound of drums and other musical instruments they toasted one another. It is not difficult to imagine their excitement and joy. But each time the emperor proposed a toast they would have to kneel down and kowtow to express their gratitude. Naturally, after the banquet everyone was exhausted.

Today, the Hall of Imperial Supremacy, and the Palace of Tranquil Longevity and its western chamber have been turned into the Exhibition Hall of Fine Arts. There is a treasure trove of paintings housed in the Forbidden City—more than 100,000 paintings executed during the period from the Jin Dynasty (265-420) to the end of the Qing Dynasty. Every year, paintings are selected from the collection to be exhibited. Throughout October, when the weather is fine and crisp, some masterpieces of paintings and calligraphy of the Jin, Tang (618-907), Song (960-1279) and Yuan (1271-1368) dynasties are exhibited, among which there are *Pingfu Rubbings (Ping Fu Tie), Spring Outing (You Chun Tu), The Imperial Carriage (Bu Nian Tu), Night Banquet (Han Xi Zai Ye Yan Tu)* and

Riverside Scene at the Qingming Festival (Qing Ming Shang He Tu).

Behind the main building of the Palace of Tranquil Longevity are the Hall of Cultivating the Character and the Hall of Joyful Longevity, living quarters for the Imperial Regent, imperial consorts and concubines. The Hall of Cultivating the Character is a smaller imitation of the Hall of Mental Cultivation. It is now the principal chamber of the Exhibition Hall of Treasures. Exhibited here are utensils, tea-services, wine pots and cups made of gold, silver or jade. There are also gold seals and gold albums. In addition, there is a set of 16 gold chimes, weighing more than 10,000 *liang* (one old *liang* equals to 31.25 g). In order to make them each sound differently, some other minerals have been blended with the gold. This set of chimes was indispensable at imperial ceremonies. There is also a gold container in which Emperor Qianlong stored strands of his mother's hair that had dropped out when she had her hair combed. It is 46 *cun* (one *cun* equals to 0.33 decimeter) high and weighs 107.5 kg. It is decorated with pearls and precious stones. Inside it there are two statues of the Buddha of Infinite Longevity.

The Hall of Joyful Longevity, also known as the Reading Chamber, behind the Hall of Cultivating the Character, was where Emperor Qianlong planned to have his study after his abdication. After Empress Dowager Cixi celebrated her 60th birthday anniversary she went to live in the western chamber of the Hall of Joyful Longevity. This was a political move, for, according to protocol, she should have retired to the Palace of Benevolence and Peace, also known as the Dowager's Dwelling. However, she regarded herself as the supreme ruler and preferred to live in the Hall of Joyful Longevity. No one dared to oppose this.

The Hall of Joyful Longevity is now the second chamber of the Exhibition Hall of Treasures. Here people can see clothes and daily necessities used by the members of the imperial house. The exhibits include Emperor Qianlong's imperial robe, the phoenix crown used as a burial object for Empress Xiaoduan of the Ming Dynasty and an ivory mat Emperor Yongzheng once slept on. There is also a huge carved jade featuring the story of Yu the Great, a mythical leader conquering the floods. It weighs 5,000 kg. It took ten years to complete this piece of superb art.

The Pavilion of Sustained Harmony, standing behind the Hall of Joyful Longevity, is now the third chamber of the Exhibition Hall of Treasures, displaying ornaments made of gold, silver, jade, precious stone, jadeite, coral and so on.

The Changyinge Stage, in the eastern part of the Palace of Tranquil Longevity, is divided into three storeys. The top floor is named the "Stage of Happiness," the middle floor, the "Stage of Wealth," and the ground floor, the "Stage of Longevity." The three floors are connected by stairs in the middle. On festival days, the occasion of a new emperor's assumption of the throne, or the birthday of an emperor or empress, local operas would be performed on this stage. Opposite the stage is the Yueshi Chamber, where the emperor, empress and other members of the imperial family sat to watch the performances. Today, performers' costumes, stage sets and pictures of opera scenes are exhibited on the ground floor of the Yueshi Chamber.

The eastern part of the Palace of Tranquil Longevity is the Qianlong Garden. Emperor Qianlong in his life made four visits to the lower Yangtze River valley and was greatly impressed by the gardens there. Therefore, he built this garden in imitation of those in the south. The garden, built between the tall wall to the west and the palaces to the east, is rather narrow. However, it was ingeniously designed to include four scenes in four areas. In the first area, there stands a pavilion which is open on four sides. This is the Guhua Chamber, surrounded by rocky hills and tall ancient trees. Opposite it is another pavilion named the Xishang Pavilion. On its floor there is a winding groove in which a stream flows. Scholars often drank while composing poems beside brooks, and it was on this notion that the Xishang Pavilion was built. A cup of wine would be placed in the groove and it would float along the water. When it stopped, the man nearest would have to drink it and compose a poem. The main structure in the second area is the Suichu Hall, a closed compound with buildings on three sides, a main building facing south and side chambers on both the east and west. It is rather roomy and bright. With ancient trees and rockeries, the whole place is tranquil and cozy.

Going further north, you come to the third and fourth areas, where there are a number of labyrinth-like structures. It is possible to get lost among these buildings.

What is worth noting behind the garden is the well inside the Zhenshun Gate and beside the Fuwang Pavilion. This is the Well of Imperial Consort Zhen. In 1900, when the Eight Allied Armies invaded Beijing, the Empress Dowager fled in a hurry. But before she did so, she ordered some eunuchs to throw Imperial Consort Zhen down this well. Visitors often linger here and sigh for the fate of the poor consort.

Having gone through the Zhenshun Gate and heading west, one comes to the Gate of Divine Might (Shenwumen), the northern entrance to the Forbidden City. Across the street towers the Prospect Hill (Jingshan). Forty-three m in height, this hill serves as a screen for the Forbidden City. This arrangement is compatible with the traditional concept of "water in front and a hill at the back" being an auspicious location.

Chapter Three
Insights into the Imperial Lifestyle

1. The Emperor's Diet and the Palace Cuisine

The emperor did not simply "eat," he "partook of viands." Ordinarily he only had two meals a day. The early meal was between 6:00 and 8:00 am, and the second was between 12:00 am and 2:00 pm. In the afternoons and evenings drinks and snacks would be served whenever the emperor felt like them. There was no fixed dining room, and the meals, etc., were served wherever the emperor happened to be.

The imperial food and beverages were specially prepared in different kitchens: the main dishes in the "imperial kitchen," cakes in the *bobo* (pastry) kitchen and tea and *naicha* (containing milk, tea,

A menu drawn up by the Imperial Viands Department.

butter and salt) in the imperial tea room. The imperial kitchen provided a different menu (Fig. 2) every day. Only when this menu had been approved by the officials of the Imperial Household Department could the food be prepared accordingly.

Eunuchs would set the table and servants from the imperial kitchen would rush the dishes to the place where the emperor was and display them in a ceremonious way. No one was allowed to eat with the emperor; even the empress and the empress dowager had to eat in their own palaces.

Each meal consisted of dozens, and sometimes more than 100 varieties of delicacies. Cakes and fruits were also served besides rice, steamed stuffed buns and other staples. The menu for Emperor Qianlong for the second day of the first lunar month in 1799 (who had retired then) is preserved in the Forbidden City. On that day at 7:30 am Qianlong breakfasted in the Hall of Mental Cultivation. Forty dishes were served, including bird's nest soup, duck, chicken, venison and pork dishes, and small steamed buns, New Year cake (made of glutinous rice flour) and other cakes. The tableware included enamel bowls, plates and saucers, sunflower-shaped jade dishes and gilded bowls. The table napkins and mats were sewn with silver thread. The late meal was similar. The leftovers were given to the eunuchs.

Like the common people, the emperor liked to eat *jiaozi* on New Year's day. In the plate of *jiaozi* one contained a silver ingot and was put on the top so that the emperor could reach it easily with his chopsticks. It was a sign of good luck. At the Lantern Festival the emperor also ate *fuyuanzi* (sweet dumplings made of glutinous rice flour).

The emperor's dining table was two-tiered. The top story was packed with dishes, which could be replaced by other dishes at any time according to the emperor's will.

Every dish and bowl contained a strip of silver as a precaution against poison. It was said that if the color of the silver changed there could be poison in the food. For the same reason, every dish was tasted by a eunuch before it was taken to the emperor. This was called "appraising the viands."

The imperial kitchen was managed by two officials of the Imperial Household Department, who spent more than 30,000 taels of silver every year on chicken, duck, fish, pork and vegetables. Rice and flour, mutton, milk and dainties of every kind were provided by the subordinate farms and pastures of the Imperial Household Department or sent as tribute by local governments. Water used by the imperial kitchen was spring water from Mount Yuquanshan in the western suburbs of Beijing. A special kind of "tribute rice" was cultivated there and at Fengzeyuan, Tangquan and other places, specially for the palace.

The food prepared for the emperor every day included: 22 *jin* of pork for dishes, 5 *jin* of pork for soup, 1 *jin* of lard, 2 sheep, 5 chickens (three of which had to be born that year), 3 ducks, 19 *jin* of Chinese cabbage, spinach, coriander, celery and Chinese chives, 60 turnips, radishes and carrots, 1 wax gourd, 6 *jin* of kohlrabi, 6 *jin* of water spinach, 6 *jin* of green onions, 4 *liang* of Yuquan wine, 3 *jin* each of two kinds of sauce, 2 *jin* of vinegar and 8 plates of *bobo*, with 30 on each plate. A plate of *bobo* needed 4 *jin* of fine wheat flour, 1 *jin* of sesame oil, 1.5 *he* (1 *he*=0.1 liter) of sesame seeds, 3 *he* of sweetened bean paste, 12 *liang* (16 *liang*=1 *jin*) of sugar, and kernel of walnut and kernel of dateplum persimmons. The imperial tea room prepared tea and milk for the emperor. There were 50 dairy cows raised specially for him, each producing 2 *jin* of milk every day. In addition, 12 pots of Yuquan water, 1 *jin* of cream and 75 packets of tea were required every day.

Sumptuous banquets were held in the Palace on New Year's Day, the Lunar New Year's Eve, the emperor's birthday and whenever the emperor entertained visiting monarchs. There were also banquets for the birthdays of the empress dowager and the empress, as well as the imperial concubines, and for the engagements and weddings of the emperor's sons and grandsons.

2. The Emperor's Grand Nuptials

The Grand Nuptials of an emperor were a complicated and extravagant process:

(1) The Presentation of the Betrothal Gifts

First, the empress dowager and the senior princes would choose a girl born into a noble family as the candidate for empress. Then the royal family would send the betrothal gifts to the girl's home, usually including horses, armor and silks. For example, the betrothal gifts for Emperor Kangxi's Grand Nuptials included "10 horses, 10 suits of armor, 100 bolts of satin and 100 bolts of cloth." Other emperors' betrothal gifts were similar.

In the early morning of that day, the gifts were placed on the steps leading to the Hall of Supreme Harmony. Two envoys and other officials, all in ceremonial dress, stood in silence, waiting for orders. As soon as the auspicious moment came, the two envoys prostrated themselves three times and knocked their heads on the ground thrice at each prostration. After that, one official would read out: "The emperor himself receives the exemplary decree from the empress dowager to take lady so-and-so as the empress. His Majesty orders you to hold the token and present the gifts." An imposing procession then set out for the residence of the future empress.

The residence of the empress was thoroughly cleaned and the whole household waited in awe for the emperor's envoys. The future empress's father had to kneel before the gate dressed in court attire to welcome them. When the envoys entered the house and the gifts were bestowed one of them declared that the betrothal gifts had been presented. The future empress's father, along with other male relatives, kowtowed in the direction of the imperial palace to show their thanks. When the whole ceremony was finished, the envoys returned to report the completion of the task.

After the presentation of the betrothal gifts, the future empress's family entertained distinguished guests and their friends, the princesses and wives of the officials entertained the future empress's mother, and the officials above the second grade invited the future empress's father to dinner.

(2) The Presentation of the Marriage Gifts

When the day of the Grand Nuptials came the imperial family

had prepared much richer gifts for the future empress's family. Usually they included 20 horses, 200 taels of gold (1 *jin*=16 taels), 10,000 taels of silver, 1,000 bolts of silk and some vessels of silver and gold. The future empress's brothers and her servants might get some costly presents, too. After the acceptance of the gifts all the male members of the family, led by the future empress's father, and the female members, led by the future empress's mother, kowtowed to show their appreciation.

(3) The Greeting Ceremony

This was the most solemn ceremony in the process of the Grand Nuptials. The whole Palace was filled with jubilation and excitement that day. The roads were covered with red felt carpets, the major palaces were decorated with red lanterns and red silk hangings bearing the "double happiness" symbol. Pictures of door gods and antithetical couplets were replaced with new ones, and even the maids and the eunuchs wore festive garments.

On the day of Emperor Guangxu's wedding, Beijing City was as festive as at the lunar New Year. All the way from the Imperial Palace to the future empress's residence—Shijia Alley in Dengshikou—was cleared of the common people and decorated. In accordance with the Qing Dynasty custom, the emperor sent officials to the Temple of Heaven, the Temple of Earth and the Imperial Ancestral Temple to offer sacrifices to the gods and ancestors one day before greeting the future empress. When the auspicious hour came, the emperor, dressed in ceremonial wedding garb, was driven in a luxurious carriage to the Palace of Benevolent Peace to salute the empress dowager. Then he took a seat in the Hall of Supreme Harmony as music and drumbeats sounded. When the music stopped the emperor cracked a whip three times, as a signal for the greeting envoy to mount the red steps to the throne and kneel down. Another official read out: "The emperor has received the order from the empress dowager to take lady so-and-so as empress. The auspicious hour has now arrived, the *huangce* (residence booklet used in the Qing Dynasty) is prepared, and His Majesty orders you to take the token and greet the empress." The grand secretary then entered the hall with the token and gave it to the greeting envoy. Another three cracks of the whip were heard, the music resumed and the emperor rose to return to his palace. At the same time, a parade of imperial guards of honor headed by the greeting envoy marched out of the Forbidden City via the Gate of Supreme Harmony and the Meridian Gate, to greet the bride.

When the parade arrived at the future empress's residence, her father and other male relatives came out and knelt before the gate to greet it. An official of the Imperial Household Department handed the future empress's bridal outfit to a eunuch, the eunuch to a woman official and she to the bride, who put it on immediately. The envoy read out the imperial decree and afterwards the future empress's father kowtowed and retreated. Then a woman official read out the imperial edict to the future empress, who knelt there listening and kowtowed when she had finished reading it. When the ceremony was over, the future empress set off for the Imperial Palace. During the Qing Dynasty there was a regulation, saying that only the emperor and the empress dowager could use the central arch of the Meridian Gate. As for the future empress, only on this occasion, i.e. on her wedding day, could she have the honor of using it. When the procession reached the Golden Stream Bridge all the officials dismounted from their horses and walked slowly across it. Bells were rung and drums were beaten when they arrived at the Meridian Gate. The bride got out of her sedan chair and walked to the Hall of Celestial and Terrestrial Union, where a peacock-roofed sedan chair carried by eight bearers (Fig. 3) was waiting to take her to the Palace of Earthly Tranquility—the bridal chamber of the emperor and empress.

(4) The Ceremony of the Nuptial Cup

This ceremony took place in the eastern chamber of the Palace of Earthly Tranquility, whose interior walls were painted red as a symbol of happiness. Besides the nuptial bed, there was a throne located in the northern part of the room. A red-lacquered screen wall was specially placed facing the door inside the room, on which a large golden Chinese character 4 meters high meaning "happi-

The imperial bridal sedan chair used to be carried by eight bearers.

ness" was pasted. So, whenever the emperor or empress opened the door to enter, he or she would first see "happiness." The bed-curtains were made of red silk, embroidered with pictures of 100 children in all poses, indicating a wish that the emperor and the empress would have many children. The floor was covered with a carpet embroidered with dragon and phoenix figures and a large "happiness" character. The last emperor, Pu Yi, described his wedding night in the chamber thus: "We entered this dark red room ... everything was red: red bed-curtains, red pillows, a red dress, a red skirt, red flowers, and a red face ... it all looked like a melted red wax candle."

With some high officials' wives gathered around, the empress entered the bridal chamber and attended to her toilet. Outside the chamber music with the themes of happiness and union marked the beginning of the ceremony. The emperor, in full ceremonial dress, was brought in a peacock-roofed sedan carried by eight bearers. He entered the chamber and seated himself on the left side of the throne, with the empress on the right, face to face. They drank the nuptial cup (two vessels were joined by a red silk thread, and the emperor drank the empress's wine and vice versa), which indicated that they would have a long life of good fortune. Outside the chamber a couple read a poem on the theme of marriage. At the same time, four high officials or princes' wives served the newlyweds with a banquet. When the feast was finished all the other people retreated, leaving the emperor and empress alone. In the evening they would eat noodles, which indicated a long life of happiness.

The cost of an emperor's wedding was enormous. Emperor Guangxu's wedding cost 5.5 million taels of silver—enough to feed 1.9 million common people for one year at that time.

After the ceremony of the Grand Nuptials, the emperor and empress would greet the empress dowager separately. The emperor would then receive congratulations from civil and military officials and foreign envoys in the Hall of Supreme Harmony. At the same time, he issued an imperial edict to announce his marriage, and then entertain the empress's parents and other officials.

3. The Selection of the Palace Harem and Lives of Concubines in the Inner Palace

Ji Xiaolan (1724-1805), a leading scholar of the Qing Dynasty, described in *An Unofficial Biography of Empress Yi An* how beauties from throughout the country were chosen for the imperial palace in the Ming Dynasty:

"In the first year of the reign of Emperor Tianqi (1621), the emperor was going to hold his Grand Nuptials ceremony. There were 5,000 beauties between 13 and 16 years old gathered in Beijing to be picked as palace maids.

"The eunuchs of the inner palace made the primary selection, rejecting 1,000 first for being a little too tall, short, fat or thin. The next day they examined each girl's ears, eyes, nose, hair, skin, neck, shoulders and back, eliminating those who had any flaws in those respects. The rest of the girls were told to announce their home-towns, names and ages. If a girl spoke with the slightest stutter or had the slightest hoarseness she would be eliminated. After these two examinations, 2,000 went home.

"On the third day of the selection, the eunuchs took measurements of the candidates' hands and feet, and ordered them to walk a short distance to observe their manners. Another 1,000 girls who had somewhat short wrists, big toes or who behaved frivolously were sent home. The 1,000 left were sent to the palace for further inspection.

"On the fourth day of selection an old palace maid led the candidates to a private room one by one. She touched their breasts, smelled their armpits and felt their skins. Only 300 were chosen this time, and these would live in the palace for one month—a period of time thought to be long enough to find out their personalities. Finally 50 girls were promoted to the position of concubine."

In the imperial families of past ages an emperor always had a large harem. A note on the *Book of Rites* records: " The Son of Heaven of the Zhou Dynasty (11th century B.C.-221 B.C.) had three empresses, nine first-ranking concubines, 27 second-ranking concubines and 81 lower-ranking concubines." In the Han (206 B.C.-A.D. 220) and Tang (618-907) dynasties there were as many as 9,000 women in the imperial harem, and the number reached 40,000 during the reign of Emperor Xuanzong of Tang. It is recorded that Emperor Jiajing of the Ming Dynasty used to select nine titled concubines at a time, with many more untitled. At the end of the Ming the number of women in the imperial harem was 9,000.

During the Qing Dynasty the number of harem inmates sharply decreased. In the reign of Emperor Kangxi the palace ladies were divided into eight ranks: an empress, a first-ranking concubine, four second-ranking, six third-ranking and other lower-ranking concubines without fixed number. Among the ten Qing emperors, Kangxi, the second one, had the most wives—55. The ninth emperor, Guangxu had the fewest, one empress and two concubines. Qianlong, the fourth emperor, who reigned for 60 years and continued in power for another three years after his ostensible resignation, (He lived to be 89, the longest-living of all the emperors) married 41 women, including girls of the Manchu, Han and Mongolian ethnic groups, as well as a Korean and a Uygur lady. Besides the concubines, there were also hundreds of serving maids living in the palace.

What was the fate of the women in the imperial palace? If a concubine fell into disfavor with the emperor, she would be forced to live in a separate palace building, perhaps for the rest of her life. Some were even murdered by eunuchs. Zhao, one of the concubines of the Ming Emperor Guangzong, is an example. Because she offended a eunuch named Wei Zhongxian, Wei forged an imperial decree, forcing her to hand over all the treasures given to her by the emperor. Finally Zhao hung herself. In the imperial palace it was very common for a concubine to be beaten to death. During the Ming Dynasty it happened that the 9,000 palace maids and the 100,000 eunuchs did not even have enough to eat, and some of them died of starvation.

4. How Did an Empress Bathe?

In the Palace people mostly used elliptical wooden tubs for bathing. The emperor's bath was prepared by eunuchs; the empress's and the concubines', by maids. Empress Dowager Cixi used two silver-coated wooden tubs: one for the upper part of her body and the other for the lower part. When She felt like bathing, eunuchs would prepare the bathtubs, water, and two trays with towels, soap and perfume on them. When the eunuchs retired, four maids attended her.

Actually it was a sponge bath. There were more than 100 towels placed in four piles on the trays. A head maid soaked the towels in lukewarm water, wrung them out, and gave one to each of the other maids. Cixi sat in a low chair and the maids rubbed her with the towels. They slowly rubbed her bosom, back, armpits and shoulders, each responsible for one part, using six or seven towels. The second step was soaping. The soap was specially made in the Palace. The maids first soaped the towels and then scrubbed Cixi's body with them. Each towel was only used once at each bathing session. In the third step the maids soaked new towels in clear lukewarm water and scrubbed Cixi all over. Anointing her with perfume was the fourth step. Each maid drenched a palm-sized piece of cloth of pure cotton with perfume and rubbed Cixi's skin with it. Finally, the four maids stroked her skin with dry towels. Altogether, 50 or 60 towels were needed for rubbing the upper part of the body. The rest were for the lower part and the process was exactly the same.

5. Where Were the Toilets?

In former days there was no special toilet in the Palace. Everyone, whether emperor, empress, concubine, maid or eunuch, used commodes (Fig. 4) or bed pans. Coal ash was used as a deodorant and to absorb moisture. The used receptacles were

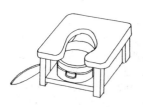

cleaned out by eunuchs and the excrement was carried out of the palace at a regular time every day. Cixi's chamber pot, known as the *guanfang*, was made of sandalwood engraved with patterns. It was wrapped in a piece of yellow cloth decorated with a cloud and dragon motif. It was brought in from outside whenever needed. In

A commode used in the imperial palace.

place of coal there were fragrant powdered wood shavings.

When Cixi felt like relieving herself, a special eunuch would carry the *guanfang* on his head to the door of the room Cixi happened to be in and unwrap it. A maid would carry it into the room, spread a piece of oilcloth on the floor and place the *guanfang* on it before inviting Cixi to use it. Cixi used tissue paper as toilet paper. When the empress dowager had finished, the maid carried the pot to the door of the room, where the eunuch wrapped it up and carried it away on his head.

6. Where Did the Water Come from?

Although there were 72 wells in the Forbidden City, ever since the reign of Emperor Qianlong the emperors always used spring water from Mount Yuquan in the western suburbs of Beijing. Every evening a donkey-cart bearing a yellow flag brought water from there to the Forbidden City via the Gate of Divine Might.

At that time, the gates of the capital closed at 10:00 pm every day. When the water cart reached the Xizhimen Gate at midnight the guards had to open the gate specially for it. The cart kept to the center of the road, and even princes and senior officials had to get out of its way.

Emperor Qianlong tasted water from every spring and well in the suburbs of Beijing and decided that the spring water from Mount Yuquan was the clearest. He gave the spring title of "First Fountain in the World." From then on, the water from this spring was exclusively for the emperor's use.

7. Keeping Warm and Cool

Beijing has a long winter. How did the imperial family keep warm?

First of all, the buildings in the Forbidden City are favorably designed to preserve heat: Most rooms face south, to catch the sunshine; thick walls and roofs keep the heat in, and the succession of walls outside the buildings serve as the first line of defence against strong winds.

There are flues under the floors of some palace rooms for space heating. In addition, there are brick beds with flues underneath in every bedroom, in which fires were made to heat them.

Since it is very cold in North China in the winter, other heating facilities were needed, mainly fire pans and braziers. These devices were elaborately decorated, some of gilded bronze and some of filigree. The small braziers could be easily held in one hand, with diameters of only 17 cm. Charcoal was used for fire pans and braziers.

The high roofs and thick walls of the halls meant that in summer it was so comfortably cool in the Forbidden City that no cooling facilities were needed. On the hottest days natural ice was put in large boxes, and bowls of food called "sweet bowls" were placed on top. In the "sweet bowl" there were lotus seeds, lotus roots and fruits, mixed with crystal sugar. These were favorite refreshments of the emperor and his concubines.

The ice was gathered in winter from the moat outside the Forbidden City and stored in an underground icehouse for use in summer.

The "refrigerator" had holes both at the bottom and on the cover so that water and cool air could circulate.

8. The Six Big Fires in the Forbidden City

In the 18th year of the Ming emperor Yongle's reign (1420), the emperor moved the capital from Nanjing to Beijing. On the following New Year's Day he received congratulations from his officials at the Hall of Worshiping Heaven (later, the Hall of Supreme Harmony). Only four months later, the three halls of the Outer Palace, known as the Three Great Halls, were struck by lightning and devoured by fire. This was regarded as an ill omen at that time. Some officials seized the opportunity to suggest moving the capital back to Nanjing. The emperor was angry at this, and had one official executed as a warning to the others. The fire damage was so extensive that the reconstruction of the Three Great Halls remained incomplete until the winter of 1441.

In the summer of the 36th year of Emperor Jiajing's reign (1557) fire destroyed the main buildings of the Outer Palace. The loss was even heavier than the previous time. The work of clearing the ruins took 30,000 laborers using 5,000 carts to complete.

The third fire took place in the 25th year of Emperor Wanli's reign (1597). The blaze not only ravaged the Outer Palace, it also reached the Palace of Heavenly Purity and the Palace of Earthly Tranquility. These disasters involved a lot of toil on the part of the common people, as they were the ones who had to clear up the mess and rebuild the ruined structures. *The History of the Ming Dynasty* records that precious trees were felled in the areas of Hubei, Hunan, Sichuan and Guizhou for timber for the rebuilding of the Three Great Halls, which cost 9.3 million taels of silver.

Besides the three big fires, another fire in the Ming Dynasty occurred in the ninth year of Emperor Zhengde's reign (1514) during the period of the Lantern Festival. Because a noble had presented special fireworks, firecrackers and lanterns to the emperor as tribute, the multicolored lanterns lit up every corner of the Palace of Heavenly Purity, and fireworks and firecrackers exploded day and night. As the emperor was making his way to the Leopard Palace accompanied by some of his harem and eunuchs, he noticed a particularly bright display and commented on it admiringly. Little did he know that one of the lanterns had fallen down and set fire to the Palace of Heavenly Purity. This blaze also reduced the Place of Earthly Tranquility to ashes.

Late at night on December 15 in the 14th year of the Qing Emperor Guangxu's reign (1888) the Zhendu Gate caught fire. Because of a strong wind, the flames quickly spread to the Gate of Supreme Harmony and the Dezhao Gate, not being put out until two days later. What had happened was that the two guards at the first gate had fallen asleep, and their lantern had set fire to the wooden pole on which it was suspended. Both guards were hanged later. The fire broke out only one month before Emperor Guangxu's wedding, during which his bride was scheduled to enter the Inner Palace through the Gate of Supreme Harmony. Since there was not enough time to rebuild the gate, a colored canopy was hastily erected.

After the 1911 Revolution the last emperor of the Qing Dynasty, Pu Yi, still lived in the Inner Palace of the Forbidden City. At that time the officials of the Imperial Household Department and the eunuchs were stealing antiques from the palace and selling them. Since the imperial household was unable to make ends meet, Pu Yi decided that an inventory should be made. At that moment, on the night of June 27, 1923, a fire broke out in the Jingsheng

Chamber in the Western Palace. A large area of buildings was destroyed, including the Palace of Central Integrity and the Chamber of Lasting Spring, where the bulk of the Forbidden City's cultural relics were stored. In his autobiography, *From Emperor to Citizen*, Pu Yi said that he suspected that the fire had been deliberately started by eunuchs to cover up their thefts. This is very likely to be true.

9. Palace Ladies Try to Assassinate the Emperor

Emperor Jiajing of the Ming Dynasty had a harsh temperament. He treated his palace ladies cruelly. They were beaten for the smallest mistakes, and altogether more than 200 of them died of ill-treatment. Eventually, on the night of the 21st day of the 10th month in the 21st year of Jiajing's reign (1542), Yang Jinying, along with 15 other palace ladies, tried to strangle the sleeping emperor. But the wrongly-tied knot was impossible to tighten, and the emperor awoke and began to struggle. Yang Jinying took a silver hairpin from her hair and stabbed the emperor with it. At the critical moment Empress Xiaolie rushed in and saved the emperor, who was already unconscious.

Yang Jinying and her 15 companions were arrested and put to death by dismemberment. Their heads were cut off and displayed in public as a warning to all. Disaster fell on their relatives as well: ten of them were executed and 20 were made slaves. It was recorded that on the day of execution a dense fog settled on the ground without abating for three or four days. People said it was a sign that an injustice was about to occur. One of the concubines, who had been sleeping with the emperor that night, was put to death in the Palace.

Although Emperor Jiajing survived the assassination attempt, he had lost an eye in the struggle. Conscious of his disfigurement, he never left the Inner Palace to appear at court again and no one from outside the palace was allowed to see his face. His grand councilor, Yan Song, was the only exception, who abused power and became a notorious treacherous court official in Chinese history.

10. Foreign Artists at the Qing Court

The Institute of Indulgences was a center in charge of court painters under the Workshop Section of the Imperial Household Department during the Qing Dynasty. Foreign artists served there and made important contributions by introducing European styles of painting to China. Lang Shining (Giuseppe Castiglione), an Italian artist, was the most famous of them. Lang was born in 1688, and in 1715 he was sent to China by the Portuguese Jesuits. He was an expert figure, flower and animal-and-bird painter. His works are lifelike and exquisite. He was the main producer of the large picture scrolls which reflected the political life of that period and proved to be of great historical value. Lang, together with other missionaries, also participated in the designing of the Yuanming-yuan, the famous royal garden in Beijing. The European-style buildings and fountains there were inspired by him. Lang lived in Beijing for more than 50 years, during which time he produced numerous paintings. In July 1766 he died in Beijing at the age of 78.

Wang Zhicheng (Jean Denis Attiret), was a French painter born in 1702. He was sent to China as a missionary in 1738 at the age of 36. It was said that Lang Shining's finding favor at the Qing Court upset the French Jesuits so much that they sent Wang Zhicheng to represent their interests in China. Because Emperor Qianlong was indifferent to oil paintings, Wang Zhicheng began to produce landscape and animal-and-bird paintings using Chinese materials. Although few of Wang Zhicheng's works survive, his *Ten Horses* is a lifelike work which shows his skill in composition. Wang Zhicheng died in Beijing in 1768 at the age of 66.

Ai Qimeng (Ignatius Sickeltart) was born in Bohemia in 1708. In 1745 he came to China as a missionary and worked at the Qing court as a painter. He painted in the Western style, favoring birds and animals as subjects. In 1777, on his 69th birthday, Emperor Qianlong held a banquet for him and bestowed on him a large amount of property. After the banquet he was carried around the city in a sedan carried by eight bearers, with a band leading the way and many officials following.

The Chinese painters working in the Institute of Indulgences were listed in the third banner of the Imperial Household Department. The foreign painters' treatment was much better than that of their Chinese colleagues. They were sufficiently supplied with meat and fruits, which was in accordance with Western dietary habits.

11. Foreigner Records the Inauguration of the Imperial Palace

When the Imperial Palace was completed Emperor Yongle of the Ming Dynasty held a grand celebration, to which many foreign envoys were invited. Gaisudin, a Persian, was one of them. In his *King Shahrukh's Envoy in China*, he, as a foreigner, for the first time described the Forbidden City and the grand occasion of the inauguration ceremony. The book was published in Chinese by the Zhonghua Book Company in 1981.

The Persian mission stayed in Beijing for a full five months, during which they were invited to the celebration of moving the capital to Beijing and the completion of the new imperial palace on the Lunar New Year's day in the 19th year of Emperor Yongle's reign.

Gaisudin records in his book that a Ming official told them: "Tomorrow is the Lunar New Year's Day, the emperor will move to the new Palace. An imperial edict forbids the wearing of any article of white clothing, because, according to Chinese tradition, people usually wear white when they are in mourning."

Gaisudin writes: "It was only at midnight that the monks came to wake us up, helped us to mount our horses and led us to the Palace, which was a magnificent group of buildings just completed after 19 years of construction. That night the houses and shops of the big city were lit up by torches, candles and lamps. It was as bright as if the sun had risen; even if an article as small as a needle fell on the ground it could not be missed. The coldness of the night seemed decreased in the brightness. Everybody was admitted to the new Palace."

He continues: "The emperor began to entertain his officials. Foreign envoys were seated outside the imperial hall (The officials below the Third Grade and the foreign envoys were seated in blue sheds built for temporary use along the west and east sides of the courtyard. — *author*). An army of 200,000 soldiers were guarding the area, with swords, clubs, halberds, spears, axes and other weapons in their hands. There were about 2,000 people, with shield-sized Chinese fans of different shapes and colors on each one's shoulder. Some adult and child actors were performing, wearing costumes that are not easy to describe in detail. Neither can my pen describe the Palace properly. To put it briefly, the distance between the gate of the main hall and the gate of the courtyard was 1,925 paces. Access to the Inner Palace was forbidden. There were palaces and halls, pavilions and gardens extending to both the west and the east. The floor of the main hall was paved with large smooth ceramic tiles, whose luster and color were very much like that of marble. The seams between the tiles were so straight that they seemed to have been drawn manually. Chinese dragons and phoenixes were engraved on the tiles, which had the luster of jade."

Apparently the white ceramic tiles in the main hall (now the Hall of Supreme Harmony) which the Persian envoy describes were not the black "gold flagstones" there today. But the Hall of Abundant Virtue, built in the Ming Dynasty and still intact today, has white glazed tiles covering the walls and the floor.

Gaisudin also writes about the officials and guests invited to the celebration: "When the emperor was seated, all the envoys lined up before the throne and kowtowed five times. Then the emperor bade them sit at their tables, on which servants placed mutton, goose, chicken, rice wine and other types of food and drink. In the meantime, acrobatic performances took place. The celebration did not finish until a ceremony was held at noon. Then the emperor rewarded the actors and rose to go to the Inner Palace. The envoys also took their leave."

12. The Attempted Murder of a Crown Prince

On the 4th day of the 5th month in the 43rd year of Emperor Wanli's reign (1615) crown prince Zhu Changluo was reading in the Ciqing Palace, when a ruffian armed with a club burst in. He attempted to attack the heir-apparent, but was arrested before he could do so. The reason for this bizarre incident, known as the "Case of the Club Attack" to history, was connected with the inheritance of the crown. Wanli's empress did not have a son, and this crown prince's mother, Wang, had been a maid serving the Empress Dowager. When she became pregnant the emperor at first denied that the child was his. But the record of the emperor's daily life said clearly: "A certain date: the maid Wang found favor with the emperor." Because he had no son at that time, the Empress Dowager urged Wanli to promote Wang to the status of concubine so that the boy Zhu Changluo could inherit the crown. Since Wang never found favor with the emperor again, Zhu Changluo was ignored by his father. When First-Ranking Concubine Zheng, who was the favorite of the emperor, gave birth to a boy, Zhu Changxun, the emperor wanted to replace Zhu Changluo with this new-born baby as the crown prince. However, his ministers were adamant that the elder son should inherit the throne, and so Zhu Changluo managed to maintain his status as crown prince.

The would-be assassin, Zhang Cha, confessed that the concubine Zheng had instigated the plot, together with two eunuchs, Pang Bao and Liu Cheng. The conspiracy had been brought to light, but the official in charge of the case dare not take any action against Zheng. He wound up the case by putting Zhang Cha to death, on the ground that he was insane. Later, Pang Bao and Liu Cheng were quietly eliminated.

13. An Heir-Apparent Raised in Secret

When Emperor Xianzong of the Ming Dynasty came to the throne at the age of 16 (in the first year of the Chenghua reign period, i.e. 1464) his 35-year-old nurse became his mistress. The maid, Wan, first slandered Xianzong's empress, Wu, so that he distanced himself from her. Next she made sure that none of the palace concubines bore a child to the emperor, by forcing them to have abortions. She herself bore a son to Xianzong in 1465, but the child died within three months.

But her plans went awry when the emperor made a woman archivist pregnant. Wan ordered her to have an abortion, but she bore the child in secret and brought him up hidden away in an obscure corner of the Forbidden City. Then one day, six years later, Emperor Xianzong lamented to a favorite eunuch that he regretted growing old without having a son to succeed him. The eunuch thereupon revealed to him the news that he did indeed have a son in the Palace. The overjoyed emperor sent for the boy at once, and the very next day announced the news to his ministers. The archivist, Ji, was promoted to the rank of concubine and moved to the Palace of Eternal Longevity.

When Wan got to know that the boy had survived she immediately started to plan her revenge. The first victim was Ji, who died mysteriously. Fearing for himself, Zhang Min, a eunuch who had helped raise the prince for the previous six years, ended his life by swallowing gold. Seeing that the little prince was in danger, the Empress Dowager took the responsibility of looking after him. Wan dared not take rash action before the Empress Dowager, but she never abandoned her intention to murder the prince. Once when Wan called the prince to go see her, the Empress Dowager warn the boy not to eat anything Wan offered him. Sure enough, when Wan urged him to eat some food, he said he was full. Then she asked him to have some soup. He said he was afraid there might be poison in it. Wan stamped her foot and cried, "How can a child say that to me? I'm sure he will kill me later." Not long after, Wan herself died.

After Emperor Xianzong died in 1487, the prince who had grown up in secret inherited the throne and became Emperor Xiaozong. The Ming Dynasty enjoyed a revival during his 18-year reign.

14. "The Cricket Emperor"

Because Zhu Zhanji, known as Emperor Xuande, was fascinated by crickets, people called him "the Cricket Emperor."

The sport of cricket fighting has a long history in China. Concubines in the Tang imperial palace liked to raise crickets in small bamboo cages. A prime minister in the Song Dynasty named Jia Sidao was such an enthusiast of cricket fighting that he neglected his duties even when the country was in dire distress. Emperor Xuande was also a cricket enthusiast. In the ninth year of his reign (1434), he issued an edict ordering Kuang Zhong, magistrate of Suzhou, to provide two eunuchs sent by the emperor with all the help they needed for collecting crickets.

The craze for raising crickets in Xuande's time was so fervent that one specimen could be worth the price of a fine horse. The story goes that a grain store supervisor in the Fengqiao area of Suzhou exchanged a fine horse for a cricket and raised it, hoping to present it to the emperor. When he was away from home his wife, curious about this valuable insect, lifted the lid from the jar it was kept in and peeped inside. The cricket suddenly jumped out and was immediately eaten by a passing rooster. The woman was so afraid of her husband's wrath that she hanged herself. When the man returned home and saw his dead wife and the empty jar he too hanged himself. It was natural that there were people at that time making fortunes or getting promotion for their skill at catching crickets.

Following the "cricket emperor," the whole country began to play with crickets, as described in a folk song: "Crickets chirp throughout the country because Emperor Xuande loves them."

15. The Empress Dowager Marries the Emperor's Uncle

Empress Dowager Xiaozhuang was the wife of Emperor Huangtaiji, an outstanding ruler in the early period of the Qing Dynasty. Since her son, Emperor Shunzhi, and her grandson, Emperor

Kangxi, both inherited the throne in their childhood, Xiaozhuang played an important role in state affairs in the early part of the Qing Dynasty.

Xiaozhuang was very beautiful and talented. When Huangtaiji came to power he sent several beautiful palace ladies to induce the Ming general Hong Chengchou to capitulate, but all in vain. At last, he sent his favorite concubine (later to become Empress Xiaozhuang). She persuaded Hong Chengchou to rescind his decision to fast to death out of loyalty to the Ming Dynasty and switch his allegiance to the Qing ruler.

Huangtaiji's untimely death made this beautiful woman a widow at the age of 30. Dorgon, Huangtaiji's brother, had been the general who had captured Beijing, and was a man of great power and influence. Because Emperor Shunzhi was only six years old, affairs in the Palace were handled by the Empress Dowager and those in the court by Dorgon. Soon after, Dorgon's wife died, and the Empress Dowager and Dorgon then got married. this was not regarded as incestuous according to Manchu custom. It is possible that Xiaozhuang agreed to the marriage in order to safeguard herself and the boy emperor in case Dorgon seized power.

16. How Emperor Kangxi Removed Aobai

Kangxi ascended the throne at the age of eight, after his father, Emperor Shunzhi died. There were four regents: Suoni, Sukesaha, Ebilong and Aobai, among whom Aobai was the lowest in rank but the most ambitious, arrogating all powers to himself.

On New Year's Day of the eighth year of Emperor Kangxi's reign, when all the ministers went to the Hall of Supreme Harmony to pay New Year greetings to the emperor, Aobai appeared in a yellow robe (no one except the emperor was allowed to wear a yellow robe in ancient China) of the same style and quality as Kangxi's. The only difference was that Aobai had a red woolen knot on his cap, while Kangxi wore a precious pearl. Another day, when Aobai pretended to be sick at home, Kangxi went to visit him and saw a dagger on his bed. According to court protocol, no one was allowed to have any weapons with him in the presence of the emperor, and so this was a serious affront to the latter.

Irritated by Aobai's arrogance, Kangxi decided to remove him. But as Aobai has many powerful allies in the court the emperor had to move cautiously. At first he pretended to be deferential to Aobai in order to put him off his guard. All this time he gathered around himself a group of youngsters who were trained in the martial arts. Then one day this group pounced on Aobai, slew his retinue and dragged him off to imprisonment. From then on, Kangxi was secure on his throne.

17. Mystery of How Yongzheng Became Emperor

Emperor Kangxi had his first son at 14. During his 61-year reign he had a total of 35 sons. The mother of the oldest, Yinti, was only a concubine, so he did not have the right to inherit the crown. The second son, Yinreng, was the son of the empress and so was naturally titled Crown Prince when he was one year old. Being the legal heir to the throne, he was brought up carefully to excel in both scholarship and military science so that he would be capable of ruling the country. However, this prince became so arrogant and domineering that he was demoted by his father when he was 34. Six months later, Kangxi restored his title, but three years later removed it again because of his recalcitrant character. Emperor Kangxi was very old at that time. His hesitation about his heir made every prince ambitious. The result was that they divided into factions to contend for the crown. Although the eighth prince, Yinsi, was the most powerful, the crown was finally grabbed by the fourth prince, Yinzhen (the later Emperor Yongzheng). Kangxi did not like this prince at all, because he was a profligate rascal who surrounded himself with low companions.

The emperor's favorite was his 14th son, whom he sent to the northwest border to temper himself in hardship. It was said that Kangxi wrote a will before he died, in which he left the throne to the 14th prince, and hid it behind a horizontal plaque bearing the words "Justice and Brightness" hung in the Palace of Heavenly

Purity. Yinzhen found out about this, and secretly changed the wording to "hand down the throne to the fourth prince."

On his deathbed Emperor Kangxi called in his senior ministers and his successor. Seeing that the fourth prince came instead of the 14th, Kangxi in a fury picked up a string of beads and threw it at him. But the cunning Yinzhen at once knelt down to thank his father, pretending that the beads were a token of the inheritor of the throne. (Another story goes that Yinzhen poisoned his father). Meanwhile, the 14th prince knew nothing of all this, being still stationed on the northwest border. And so the rightful heir to the throne was cheated of his inheritance.

18. Cixi's Wealth and Her Extravagance in Dining

In her later years Cixi (Fig. 5) became extremely avaricious. At that time the Imperial Household Department allocated her 200,000 taels of silver for food every month. But instead of spending this money, she horded it in nine storerooms next to her living quarters. At least every other day she would go there to fondle her gold, silver, jewellery and other treasures. No one knows how much wealth she actually had. When the storerooms were looted in 1900 by the Allied Forces of the Eight Powers, Cixi's first thought upon returning to Beijing was to fill them again. Cixi's 65th birthday happened to be coming up, so she issued an edict to the governors of the richest provinces, informing them that central officials would go to inspect their finances right after her birthday. These provinces understood the real purpose behind the edict, and each paid enormous tribute as birthday gifts. The viceroy of Liangjiang (an area covering Jiangsu, Anhui and Jiangxi provinces) sent four gold figurettes, weighing more than 60 jin each, plus a string of 108 precious beads; the governor of Anhui Province sent 100,000 silver coins. The governor of Jiangxi presented 1,000 British golden guineas, and the head of the Shanghai Customs sent a pair of shoes ornamented with numerous diamonds, rubies, emeralds and other jewels. The richest gift was presented by Yuan Shikai, Governor of Zhili (the name of a former province, referring to areas including

The Empress Dowager Cixi (middle), who ruled China for half a century, receives foreign diplomatic envoys' wives.

Beijing, Tianjin, part of Hebei, Liaoning and Inner Mongolia), who gave 30,000 gold coins.

Beside gold and silver, every year Cixi received 96 bolts of high-quality silks and satins, 50 bolts of cotton cloth and 124 furs of various kind from the Imperial Household Department.

In addition, there was a special convention that the gold and silver articles and porcelain wares that the Empress Dowager used be replaced with new ones every year, which included 36 golden articles such as candlesticks, kettles, cups and spoons, 135 silver articles and 1,026 pieces of porcelain.

Cixi was served with more than 100 dishes every day. Tables decorated with gold flowers were set before her, and dozens of eunuchs carried the dishes into the palace in sequence, placing the dishes that the Empress Dowager favored near her and others somewhat further off. Actually only a few dishes were touched; the others were just for display. The tableware consisted of more than 1,500 pieces.

Her supper on one Lunar New Year's day was attended by "four guardian warriors" and "500 arhats." In fact, the "four guardian warriors" were four retired eunuchs who had good service records and had been called in specially for this grand occasion. The "arhats" were 500 eunuchs in uniform lined up from the entrance of the palace to the Imperial Viands Room. They had been carefully selected, neither too old nor too young. These eunuchs had been strictly trained to move smoothly and quickly with a tray on one palm.

Cixi was accompanied by Emperor Guangxu and the empress. There were three tables of dishes called "Heaven," "Earth" and "Man," respectively. Putting her palms together, Cixi at first faced east to salute Heaven, then west to salute Earth and at last seated herself at the middle table. This suggested that besides Heaven and Earth, she was the only one to be respected. When Cixi sat down, the "four guardian warriors" came up to greet her, and the "500 arhats" began to shout together: "We wish the Old Buddha (Li Lianying, a chief eunuch, was the first one to call Cixi the 'Old Buddha') a long life!" The whole palace then bustled with excitement and the sound of firecrackers.

The dishes were divided into three categories: the first were dishes bearing auspicious names; the second, dainties of every kind sent by the localities; the last, regular dishes made by the Imperial Kitchen for a holiday celebration. The emperor sat on Cixi's left and the empress sat on her right. Every time the emperor picked up food for Cixi, the empress would recite the name of the dish, which had been announced by the eunuchs when it had been served.

19. Cixi Intercedes for the Empress

It was Cixi who insisted that Longyu become Guangxu's empress. The couple were never happy together, nor did they have any children.

Once on New Year's Day, when Cixi was having tea after the

evening feast, Emperor Guangxu went to pay his regular courtesy call on her.

Cixi asked: "Where have you come from?"

Guangxu answered, "From the Hall of Mental Cultivation."

"Via the Zhongsi Gate?"

"Yes."

"Do you know the interpretation of the Zhongsi Gate?"

"Your humble son is not diligent in learning. Would you please teach me something about it?"

Zhongsi means grasshopper in Chinese. This insect is renowned for its immense reproductive capacity, and the purpose of naming a gate after it was to wish the imperial family many offspring. Empress Longyu was Cixi's niece and it was Cixi who made her the empress. Seeing that the emperor and the empress did not go on well together, Cixi worried that they would not have a son. It was obvious that her allusion to the Zhongsi Gate was a suggestion that Guangxu should take steps to produce a son as soon as possible.

She told the emperor: "When our ancestors entered Beijing they changed the names of many of the Ming buildings, but left that of the Zhongsi Gate. They hoped the imperial family of Qing would grow. It is said that when a male grasshopper flaps his wings and chirps, a group of female insects will gather around, each giving birth to 99 more grasshoppers. It was our ancestors' wish for a flourishing family."

But Cixi's concern was all in vain; Empress Longyu never gave birth.

20. The Empress Dowager's Cruelty

When Emperor Tongzhi prepared his Grand Nuptials at the age of 17, daughters of Mongolian and Manchu officials were selected as candidates for empress and imperial consorts.

Tongzhi's mother, Empress Dowager Cixi, favored the daughter of Fengxiu, while Tongzhi and Empress Dowager Ci'an liked the daughter of Chongqi. At last, Chongqi's daughter became the empress and Fengxiu's daughter served as imperial consort. Cixi then constantly tried to get the emperor to neglect the official empress in favor of the imperial consort. But the result was that Tongzhi ended up neglecting both of them. He slept alone in the Palace of Heavenly Purity, where he indulged in all kinds of vices. He was encouraged in this by his eunuchs, who would even smuggle him out of the palace in disguise to visit brothels. Before long, he was infected with venereal disease.

When the Imperial Physician was sent for, he immediately understood what disease the emperor had caught. Afraid to speak frankly, he asked the Empress Dowager: "What does Your Majesty think the emperor's disease is?" Cixi, afraid that the shameful news would become public, replied casually: "Perhaps it's smallpox." The doctor took the hint at once. "Your Majesty has wise judgment; it seems to be smallpox." Because Tongzhi did not get the right treatment, a few days later his disease got worse.

The pregnant empress herself came to attend him. Knowing that he was in danger of death, Tongzhi scribbled a note bequeathing the throne to her baby if it should be a boy. Just at that moment, Cixi burst in, snatched the note and burned it in the flame of an oil lamp. The empress fled, and Tongzhi died later the same day, possibly suffocated by Cixi herself.

Cixi later went so far as to blame the empress for the emperor's death. The distraught empress thereupon tried to kill herself by swallowing gold, but was discovered and revived. Afraid that the pregnant empress would give birth to a boy, who would naturally become the emperor, and, as a result, the empress would replace her as the empress dowager, Cixi secretly ordered that the empress be slowly starved to death. Finally, late at night on February 20, 1875, Tongzhi's empress committed suicide. All three, the young couple and their unborn baby, had been persecuted to death by the cruel Empress Dowager Cixi.

21. Friction Between the East Empress Dowager and the West Empress Dowager

When the East Empress Dowager of the Qing Dynasty, Ci'an,

had been made empress, the later West Empress Dowager, Cixi, had just entered the Palace. She had been selected as a low-ranking concubine by Emperor Xianfeng, who doted on her very much, sometimes to the neglect of affairs of state.

One day, Empress Ci'an called Cixi to the Palace of Earthly Tranquility, and berated her for leading the emperor astray. She was about to inflict corporal punishment upon her with a cane, when Emperor Xianfeng hurried in and begged her not to, saying that Cixi was pregnant. Since Cixi gave birth to a son (who later became Emperor Tongzhi) by Emperor Xianfeng, she was promoted three times, and at last became an empress dowager, the same rank as Ci'an. After Emperor Xianfeng died, in August 1861, the two empress dowagers cooperated to suppress attempts to usurp the throne by the "eight grand ministers" and became co-regents as Emperor Tongzhi was still a minor. Though Cixi showed more affection for Ci'an after that, addressing her as "my sister," the two of them had brushes in private.

One of the sources of conflict between them was the profligate behavior of the young widow Cixi. Another was Ci'an's insistence that her co-regent treat her as senior in rank. Once, when the two of them went to Emperor Xianfeng's tomb to hold a memorial ceremony, Cixi wanted to stand side by side with Ci'an. But the latter publicly insisted that Cixi remain a few paces behind. This was a humiliation for Cixi, and she harbored a grudge against Ci'an.

Cixi sent her most trusted eunuch, An Dehai, to have the emperor's robes made in an area located south of the lower reaches of the Yangtze River. This was a violation of the court protocol as eunuchs were prohibited from leaving the capital, on pain of death. An Dehai not only left the capital, but acted in such an oppressive manner that complaints were made to Empress Dowager Ci'an. She immediately ordered that An Dehai be executed, ignoring all Cixi's pleading on his behalf.

Fearing that Cixi would bully Ci'an when the former's son

became the emperor after he died, Emperor Xianfeng wrote a secret edict to Ci'an on his deathbed, giving her the right to punish Cixi if she broke court discipline. Ci'an kept the edict hidden for two years. But then, fooled by Cixi's apparent affection, she not only showed the edict to Cixi, but burned it in her presence to prove her trust in her. However, though Cixi pretended to be grateful, she did not cease to regard Ci'an as a rival, and continued to plot against her.

In March of the seventh year of Guangxu's reign, Ci'an suddenly died, at the age of 35. Rumors spread quickly. One said that Ci'an died just a few hours after eating a piece of cake sent by Cixi; another said that she had partaken of a bowl of soup cooked by Cixi. The real cause of her death is a mystery.

22. The Tragedy of Concubine Zhen

Emperor Guangxu had a smaller harem than any other Qing emperor, only an empress and two concubines. The two concubines, Jin and Zhen, were sisters. The latter, who was young, beautiful, lively, and fond of dressing up as a boy, was Guangxu's favorite. She helped the emperor in his attempts to reform the political system and govern wisely, but thereby incurred the wrath and jealousy of Cixi.

In August, 1900 when the Allied Forces of the eight Powers occupied Beijing, Cixi forced Emperor Guangxu to flee to Xi'an with her. Before she went she ordered the chief eunuch, Cui Yugui, to fetch Concubine Zhen to her and said to her: "The Westerners are going to enter the city. If they humiliate you, it will be a disgrace to our imperial family. I will not be able to account for this to our ancestors."

She then ordered Cui Yugui to throw Concubine Zhen down a nearby well.

This well is located in the northeastern corner of the Forbidden City. Because it was where Concubine Zhen died, it is called the Concubine Zhen Well.

23. Anecdotes of the Last Emperor

After the Manchu forces conquered China and established the Qing Dynasty, they forced all men of the Han nationality to wear their hair in pigtails. For more than 200 years, the penalty for not doing so was beheading. Toward the end of the dynasty, revolutionary pioneers began to cut off their pigtails to show their determination of overthrowing the power of the Qing Dynasty. Pu Yi, who was influenced by his English teacher Reginald F. Johnston, also disliked men's pigtails. He cut out his own regardless of the objections of the princes and his ministers. Of course the emperor would have many followers. In a few days, about a thousand pigtails in the Forbidden City were cut out, except that Pu Yi's Chinese teacher Chen Baochen and several Imperial Household Department officials remained their pigtails and took them to their coffins.

Pu Yi was a lazy student. One of his favorite pastimes was watching busy ants. He would squat for hours under a tree watching them. Because Pu Yi refused to learn his lessons, his teacher had to ask the chief eunuch, Zhang Qianhe, to recite them. As a teenager, Pu Yi was obsessed with new toys. When he was learning to ride a bicycle, he had all the thresholds removed from the palace gates so that he could get through them without obstacles. He asked the Imperial Household Department to buy models of all the famous bicycles in the world for him. When he got bored with one, he would give it to a servant and then demanded a new one. He always had more than 20 bicycles at a time. Later, when Pu Yi fell in love with automobiles, he bought three at the same time.

Pu Yi also enjoyed raising dogs, of which he had more than 100, each with a plaque round its neck with its name and number on it. He spared no expense to buy Western dogs at high prices. German police dogs were his favorites.

Pu Yi later became very impressed by his British teacher. He wore Western-style clothes, ate Western food, rode bicycles, played tennis, wore glasses, installed a telephone in the Palace and, like his teacher, used English words. He even thought of going to Britain to study. Wan Rong, Pu Yi's empress also had a British teacher to teach her English. She was not only able to speak and write in English, but also called herself Elizabeth.

24. Connotations of the Motifs on the Imperial Robe and the *Bufu*

The emperor's robe was called the dragon robe (or python robe). Nine golden dragons were embroidered on it, each having five claws. One of the dragons was hidden inside; only when the front of the robe was opened could people see it.

The imperial robe was decorated with gold lace. It had a low, round collar, horseshoe-shaped cuffs and a front flap fastening under the right shoulder. The robe was long enough to reach the ground. Embroidered on the chest was a dragon clutching a pearl, with other dragons surrounding it. Other decorations were symbolic waves and mountains. The composition indicated the emperor's power over the whole country and the eternal peace and prosperity of society under his rule.

During the Qing Dynasty officials wore robes with silk patches embroidered with specific motifs on the chest and the back. These robes were called *bufu*. Those motifs were used to indicate the different ranks of official. Birds indicated civil officials, and beasts stood for military officers. For the civil officials, the symbol of the top rank was a red-crowned crane; that of the second, a golden pheasant; that of the third, a peacock; the fourth, a skylark; the fifth, a silver pheasant; the sixth, an egret; the seventh, a *xichi* (a kind of aquatic bird mentioned in ancient books); the eighth, a quail; and the ninth, a long-tailed flycatcher. (Fig. 6)

For the military officers, the top rank was indicated by a *kylin* (Chinese unicorn); the second, a lion; the third, a leopard; the fourth, a tiger; the fifth, a bear; the sixth, a *biao* (young tiger); the seventh and the eighth, a rhinoceros; and the ninth, a sea horse. (Fig. 7)

The designs embroidered on the *bufu* (the patch on the front of an official robe marking one's rank) of civil officials' robes. From top left to bottom right are the designs from the first to the ninth ranks.

The beast designs embroidered on the *bufu* of military officials' robes. From top left to bottom right are the designs from the first to the ninth ranks. The designs of the seventh and eighth ranks are the same.

25. How Many Rooms Are There in the Forbidden City?

There are 9,999.5 rooms in the Forbidden City. This strange number makes people wonder why there are not 10,000 rooms and what the half-room looks like.

It was said that the legendary Jade Emperor (the Supreme Deity of Daoism) owned 10,000 rooms in Heaven. Since the human emperor was believed to be the son of the emperor in Heaven, it was natural for a son to be inferior to his father, the imperial family could build at most 9,999.5 rooms.

The half-room lies at the western end of the ground floor of the Wenyuan Chamber. In fact, it was built to complement the major structure.

No one knew in which room and on which bed the emperor would sleep each night, except his closest eunuchs. This was a precaution against assassination. As a matter of interest, it has been calculated that, sleeping in a different room every night, it would take 27 years to sample all the rooms in the Forbidden City.

26. Corner Towers of the Forbidden City

There are four towers exactly alike standing at the four corners

This is one of the watchtowers set on each of the four corners of the wall surrounding the Forbidden City.

of the Forbidden City. (Fig. 8) They are ancient fortifications built both for defense and ornamentation. The corner towers were constructed during the Ming Dynasty, in Emperor Yongle's reign (1403-1424). The total height of each tower from the ground is 27.5 m. The part above the wall of the Forbidden City, with railings of white marble around it, was exquisitely made of first-class *Phoebe nanmu*. The eaves of the towers curve upward, giving the buildings a soaring grace.

There is a legend about the corner towers of the Forbidden City: The emperor gave his craftsmen only nine days to design them. Eight days passed, and they still had no idea about the design. As they cudgeled their brains, sitting in a teahouse, an old peddler came up and tried to sell them a cricket cage. When the impatient craftsmen ordered him to be off, the old man smiled a cunning smile and said, "Look carefully. This is not a cage just anyone can make." Then he pointed out to them the cage's exquisite workmanship: It had nine beams, 18 columns and 72 ridges. So they took it as the model for the towers. The old man was not an ordinary person, according to the story, but the master carpenter Lu Ban who became an immortal.

27. Stage Plays in the Imperial Palace

Stage plays and operas were some of the most important forms of entertainment in the Forbidden City. Holidays and ceremonial occasions such as the accession of a new emperor, the birthday of an emperor or empress, and especially New Year's Day, the Dragon Boat Festival, the Mid-autumn Festival and the Double Ninth Festival, saw the staging of lavish performances.

The office in charge of stage performances in the imperial palace was called *jiaofangsi* (the Music Office) in the Ming Dynasty and *shengpingshu* (the Court Theatrical Office) in the Qing Dynasty.

The Changyinge Stage in the courtyard of the Yueshi Chamber behind the Palace of Tranquil Longevity was where the emperor and empress, princes and ministers watched performances. Most of the dramas were about kings, ministers and generals, or supernatural deities. The central theme was one of applauding the merits of the ruler, who brought his country prosperity and peace.

Every actor performing in the palace lived in constant fear of death for offending the emperor accidentally. The book *Miscellany of the Whistling Pavilion* records such a story. Once an actor playing the role of the governor of Changzhou was rewarded by Emperor Yongzheng for his excellent performance. In his elation the actor went so far as to ask the emperor who the governor of Changzhou at that time was. For this act of lese-majeste, the actor was beaten to death.

Chen Delin was a Beijing opera actor who was once called to the palace to perform *The Story of Su San, the Courtesan*. There is a line in the play which goes: "The sheep captured by a tiger will never return." Since Cixi, who was watching the performance, was born in the Year of the Sheep, Chen, in order not to displease the empress dowager, changed the words to: "The fish which falls into a net will never return." It was his quick wit that saved his life.

28. The Bronze Lions of the Forbidden City

There are six pairs of bronze lions in the Forbidden City, of which the pair in front of the Gate of Supreme Harmony are the largest. Originally lions were sent to the Han Dynasty emperors as tribute by the Anxi Kingdom. Their brave and noble countenances were often used in paintings and statues as decorations in ancient architecture. Among the six pairs of lions in the Forbidden City, five are gilded and glitter when the sun shines. Bronze lions were placed in the Forbidden City as a symbol of dignity and grace rather than as decorations. The lions placed in front of gates are not exactly the same, but are distinguished by the bumps on their heads: The bronze lions placed in front of the residence of a first-ranking official had 13 bumps on their heads, and the number decreased according to the official's rank, until the number reaches eight. Officials lower than the seventh rank were not allowed to have lions outside their gates.

The six pairs of lions of the Forbidden City made during the Ming and Qing dynasties are very lifelike, each sitting on a platform, mouth open, as if they are roaring. The strong claws reflect their unconquerable personalities.

In each pair of lions, the female, on the right, is stretching out her left leg to play with a baby lion, who is lying on its back, with its mother's claws in its mouth, revealing the maternal love of the mother lion for her baby. The male lion, on the left, is playing with a ball with his right leg, as if he is performing the traditional lion's dance.

29. The Bronze Vats for Fire Protection

Big bronze vats can be observed in the courtyards in the inner palace and along the east and west axes of the Forbidden City. They were used both for decoration and for fire protection. In the past the vats were always filled with water, ready at any moment to be used in case of fire. In winter the vats would be insulated with a cotton-padded covering, lidded and heated underneath by a fire on the stone platform to keep the water in the vats from freezing.

During the Ming Dynasty most of the vats were made of iron or bronze, while in the Qing Dynasty all were gilded bronze vats. A vat with a diameter of 1.6 m weighs about 3,392 kg and one with a diameter of 1.28 m weighs about 2,166 kg. One of the bigger vats would cost more than 500 taels of silver to make.

When the Allied Forces of the eight Powers occupied Beijing in 1900 the gold was scraped off the vats. The stripped vats can still be seen in the Palace Museum.

30. What Is the Significance of the Number of the Gate Nails?

Every gate in the Forbidden City has golden nails in it to keep the boards in place.

The south gate (the Meridian Gate), the north gate (the Gate of Divine Might) and the west gate (the Western Flowery Gate) have 81 nails, each arranged in a 9 by 9 formation. Since 9 is the biggest yang number (odd number) smaller than 10, the 9 by 9 style was regarded as the highest-ranking placement of nails. The only exception is the east gate of the Forbidden City (the Eastern Flowery Gate), in which there are only 72 nails, in 8 by 9 formation. One explanation for this is that the Eastern Flowery Gate was a "ghost gate," through which an emperor's coffin would be carried out of the Forbidden City to be kept on Coal Hill when he had passed away. But this is not convincing, for the emperors also went out through this gate on royal tours. The real explanation remains a mystery.

During the Qing Dynasty there was clear rule about the number of the nails in a gate. *The Comprehensive Law of the Great Qing Dynasty* regulates that the gate of a palace, a temple or an altar should be painted red and have golden nails in it, in 9 by 9 formation; and the gate of a residence of a prince should have nails in 7 by 9 formation. Since the number of the nails was a mark of one's rank, anyone daring to transgress it would be punished.

31. Mosaics in the Imperial Garden

In the Imperial Garden of the Forbidden City there is a one-km-long path paved with mosaics, containing more than 720 pictures and continuous patterns. The contents of the pictures range from flowers, people, birds and beasts to folk customs and historical stories. For example, a picture named *Seal Hung Up and Robe Given Away* tells a story which dates from the period of the Three Kingdoms (220-265). In the picture, the famous general Guan Yu is on horseback holding a sword, on the top of which is hanging a green embroidered brocade robe. A man kneels before him holding a tray carefully in his hands, whose extreme deference is caught exactly in the picture.

Another picture tells the story of *The Weasel Paying His Respects to the Hen*, which is not only lifelike but also pregnant with meaning. In the picture a sly weasel is paying his respects to a big fat hen, who glares at him and clucks to warn her children of danger. The chickens flutter about looking for refuge.

Afraid of My Wife, one of the pictures reflecting the life of ordinary people, shows a husband kneeling before his wife's foot with an oil lamp on his head. *A Hundred Seeds in A Split Pomegranate* is meant to be auspicious. Many seeds can be seen when a ripe pomegranate splits naturally. This is a symbol of a flourishing population.

Chapter Four

The 24 Ming and Qing Emperors Who Lived in the Forbidden City

1. Emperor Chengzu—Zhu Di (1360-1424)

Zhu Di, who reigned from 1402 to 1424, was the fourth son of Zhu Yuanzhang, the founding emperor of the Ming Dynasty.

Emperor Chengzu

Zhu Di was first conferred the title the Prince of Yan and given the command of the guard of Beiping. A resourceful and astute man, he frequently dispatched his troops to outlying areas to defeat the remaining forces of the Yuan Dynasty.

Once when Zhu Yuanzhang asked his grandson, Zhu Yunwen (the son of the emperor's eldest son), if he could match a line of poetry which read, "When the wind blows, the horse's tail fans out like a thousand threads." Zhu Yunwen responded, "When the rain falls, the lambs emit a strong stench." On hearing this, Zhu Yuanzhang was very displeased because, though there was nothing wrong with the verse structure, it sounded unbearably vulgar to him. Zhu Di, who was standing by, quickly offered a line of his own, which read, "When the sun shines, the scales of the dragon become like ten thousand points of gold." To everyone present, it sounded both more poetic and graceful, and brought instant praise from Zhu Yuanzhang, who had not realized that Zhu Di was a man versed in letters as well as the martial arts, decided to change the rule of succession which made his first grandson, Zhu

75

Yunwen, his successor by making Zhu Di his successor instead. It was only after fervent pleas by his ministers against any change in the law of primogeniture, which held that the eldest son or the first grandson of the eldest son should be made successor, was his order rescinded. He had no choice but to make Zhu Yunwen his successor.

Upon the death of Zhu Yuanzhang, Zhu Yunwen ascended the throne and ordered the princes of the vassal states not to journey to Nanjing (the capital at that time) for the funeral. Ignoring this order, Zhu Di set out for Nanjing. When Zhu Yunwen learned of this, he ordered the garrison at Huai'an, in today's Jiangsu Province, to turn Zhu Di back. This further intensified the enmity between the uncle and the nephew. In the first year of his reign Zhu Yunwen attempted to consolidate his power by weakening that of the vassal states, thereby weakening his uncles, who had been made princes of several vassal states during the reign of his grandfather. Zhu Di, feeling threatened, decided to enlarge his armies secretly, while pretending to be sick and feigning madness. This was to confuse Zhu Yunwen. When the time came, Zhu Di declared a state of emergency and led his armies south to Nanjing. The war between uncle and nephew lasted for more than four years. It came to be known as the "Jingnan (Pacifying the Misfortune) Incident." In June 1402 Zhu Di captured Nanjing and the throne. Zhu Yunwen set himself afire and burned to death in the palace. In the following year Zhu Di gave his reign the title of "Yongle (Forever Happy)."

His reign began with rampant revenge killing. Most of the eunuchs, maids and others who had served the former emperor were killed within a few days. Once when Zhu Di ordered Fang Xiaoru, a literary scholar who had served Zhu Yunwen, to write a proclamation of enthronement, Fang, a loyal servant of his former master, threw his writing brush onto the floor in defiance. "You may not be afraid of death," challenged Zhu. "But aren't you afraid that your clan to the ninth degree of kinship will be killed as well?" Fang replied sternly, "Even if you wipe out my entire family I will never write it!" After saying this, he wrote four Chinese characters on a piece of paper and threw it at Zhu. It read, "The thief of Yan has stolen the throne." (Zhu Di had been originally the prince of Yan.) Zhu Di was enraged and ordered Fang's mouth slashed from ear to ear. Then he had the homes of Fang's family, relatives, friends and even students searched and had 873 of such people, ten clans altogether, killed one by one before Fang in an attempt to make him change his mind. But Fang stood and watched all of them killed without consenting to write the proclamation.

Jing Qing, another devoted servant of Zhu Yunwen's, tried to assassinate Zhu Di. His family also met with disaster. This sort of punishment of killing all of an enemy's family and relatives and friends, initiated by Zhu Di, was known as "uprooting the creeping vine."

As for other people loyal to the former emperor, whom Zhu Di needed to carry on running the court, he destroyed in public all the documents and memorials they had submitted to the former emperor. "You are my subordinates now," said Zhu Di. "As long as you are loyal to me, we can allow the past to remain in the past."

His empress was the eldest daughter of Xu Da, one of the leading figures at the founding of the Ming Dynasty. When she died, Zhu Di decided to make her sister, Xu Miaojin, the new empress, but the latter was strongly opposed to this. In protest, she shaved her head and became a Buddhist nun. Zhu Di had no choice but to give up this idea. No other empress was installed during Zhu Di's reign.

Zhu Di was an emperor with some achievements to his name. He built water conservancy projects and encouraged both agriculture and the handicrafts industry. In the third year of Yongle (1405), Zhu Di sent an envoy named Zheng He to the Western Seas to promote friendship and trade relations with over 30 countries. He also led five campaigns to the north to quell threats from pockets of resistance left over from the Yuan Dynasty. After Zhu Di expanded the city of Beijing and moved the capital there he oversaw the restoration of the Great Wall. He also organized the compiling of *The Great Encyclopedia in the Reign of Emperor Yongle*, the first and most comprehensive encyclopedia in Chinese history.

Zhu Di died while on a northern expedition in July 1424. Buried with him were 30 maids of honor, who were feted with a banquet and then forced to stand on a wooden bed with ropes around their necks. The bed was then pulled out from under them.

2. Emperor Renzong—Zhu Gaochi (1378-1425)

Zhu Gaochi was the eldest son of Zhu Di. When Zhu Di attacked Nanjing he made Zhu Gaochi stay in Beiping to gard the city. With only 10,000 troops, he fought off as many as 500,000

Emperor Renzong

soldiers of Emperor Jianwen. He was responsible for the capital garrison during Zhu Di's many northern expeditions. Known as a generous man, once when passing through Zouxian County en route to Beiping, he saw people picking wild herbs in a field. He stopped to investigate and visited their homes. When he learned they had been made destitute by a series of natural disasters he ordered his eunuchs to distribute food and money to them.

Nevertheless, it was Zhu Gaoxu and Zhu Gaosui, the two brothers of Zhu Gaochi, whom Zhu Di favored more. In fact, Zhu Di once planned to remove him from the position of crown prince, instigated by the two brothers. But when Zhu Di realized that it was a plot he gave up the idea of replacing Zhu Gaochi as crown prince.

In 1424 Zhu Di died, and Zhu Gaochi succeeded to the throne. In the following year he titled his reign "Hongxi." But he died only one year after taking power, at the age of 48.

When Zhu Gaochi was on throne he ordered the release and rehabilitation of some officials who had served Emperor Jianwen.

Their duties and titles were restored, and their advice respected. He even sometimes criticized himself in public. Also, he recognized the plight of the poor and adopted relief policies. He cracked down on corrupt officials. As a result, his subjects enjoyed peaceful lives. Keen on studying, Zhu Gaochi often discussed classical works and history with his officials.

3. Emperor Xuanzong—Zhu Zhanji (1398-1435)

The eldest son of Zhu Gaochi (Emperor Renzong) was named the crown prince when Renzong took the throne. He was sent to garrison Nanjing when an earthquake occurred and urgently summoned back to Beijing when Renzong fell seriously ill. As soon as the envoy who had been dispatched to call him back arrived in Nanjing, the news of his father's death came. On his way back to Beijing, he was informed that his uncle, Zhu Gaoxu, had planned an ambush. He still proceeded northward despite the danger, and the ambush never took place.

Emperor Xuanzong

As soon as he arrived at the palace he took the throne. He titled his reign "Xuande" in 1426, the year following his enthronement. He reigned for 11 years before he died at the age of 38.

As emperor, he retained most of the officials from his father's court and got along well with them. He distanced himself from those that he found to be corrupt and surrounded himself with those that he could trust. During his reign Kuang Zhong, prefect of Suzhou, a well-known official respected for his honesty and forthrightness was one such person trusted by the emperor. Xuanzong carried out a policy of poverty relief through tax exemptions and aid to poverty stricken areas. He led a simple life and cut the size of his staff and court officials to further reduce the tax burden on the poor. For most of his reign life was peaceful and society was relatively stable.

In August 1426 Zhu Gaoxu led a mutiny in the ancient city of Yue'an, in today's Guangrao County, Goangdong Province. Zhu Zhanji quelled the uprising and captured Zhu Gaoxu. Zhu Zhanji's staff urged him to put Zhu Gaoxu to death. He rejected their suggestion and placed him under house arrest instead. A few years later a plea for his release was ignored by Zhu Zhanji. Then, Emperor Xuanzong came to see him, Zhu Gaoxu refused to kowtow. The emperor reprimanded him and was about to leave when Zhu Gaoxu tripped him with his outstretched foot. The emperor had a 150kg copper jar placed over him, but Zhu Gaoxu was a very strong man, and he was able to move the jar. Xuanzong then ordered hot coals placed around the jar. Zhu Gaoxu was eventually roasted to death.

Xuanzong had not produced a son by the age of 30. According to legend, one of his concubines, Sun, informed the emperor that she was pregnant. Eight months later she snatched a baby boy from a palace servant and told the emperor that it was their son. Naturally, Xuanzong was very pleased and was unaware that he had been deceived. Four months later he named the baby crown prince and made Sun his empress. The purloined infant was to become the Emperor Yingzong.

Society was relatively stable under the reigns of Renzong and Xuanzong, which came to be known in history as the "Reign of Ren-Xuan."

4. Emperor Yingzong—Zhu Qizhen (1427-1464)

The eldest son of Emperor Xuanzong, Zhu Qizhen succeeded to the throne in 1435, when Xuanzong died, and titled his reign Zhengtong. As the sixth emperor of the Ming Dynasty, he was on the throne for 22 years and died at the age of 38.

Zhu Qizhen was only nine when he took the throne. But with the assistance of experienced officials, the state enjoyed stability. After the empress and many of the old officials died, his favorite

Emperor Yingzong

was his teacher, Wang Zhen, who was later promoted to the position of eunuch in charge of ceremonies, a position that he swiftly abused. This man's corruption and dismissal of the old officials on whom the young Zhu Qizhen had relied so heavily led to increasing instability.

In 1449 Ye Xian, head of the Wala tribe of Mongolia, led his troops southward to attack the border and occupied the city of Datong. Because Wang Zhen was concerned that his private property would be seized in his hometown of Weizhou, a small city near Datong, he saw that no effort was spared to make Zhu Qizhen lead 500,000 troops against the enemy. Inadequate training and poor command led to exhaustion and the eventual defeat of the imperial army at Tumubao, about 10 km east of today's Huailai County in Hebei Province. When Emperor Yingzong was surrounded by the enemy, and with his soldiers falling all around him, General Fan Zhong pointed to Wang Zhen and said, "We have you to blame for this: one emperor besieged and soldiers slaughtered. Today you shall pay with your life." As he said this, he raised his mace and struck Wang Zhen dead. In one last effort, the general tried to lead the troops to break through the encirclement, but to no avail. When Yingzong saw General Fan Zhong killed, he resigned himself to defeat. He dismounted from his horse and sat on the ground to await death. But he was captured alive and taken to the north. This episode, known as the "Incident at Tumubao," marked the beginning of the decline of the Ming Dynasty.

The dynasty could not be without an emperor for even one day. Therefore, Zhu Qiyu (Daizong), who was left to defend Beijing, took the throne. But in 1405, when Yingzong was released, Daizong would not relinquish power. Instead, he only granted

Yingzong the title of overlord, and forced him to live in what was known as the Southern Palace in today's Duanku Lane at Nanchizi, in the center of Beijing.

In the first lunar month of 1457 Zhu Qiyu became seriously ill. One night, General Shi Heng, Minister Xu Youzhen and the eunuch Cao Jixiang with their men and broke into the Southern Palace, and freed the imprisoned Yingzong. He was taken from there by carriage to the Hall of Heavenly Worship (Today's Hall of Supreme Harmony in the Forbidden City) and made emperor once again. Chimes and drums were sounded, officials were called before him, and his restoration to the throne announced. This is known as the "Incident of Breaking the Gate."

After his restoration, he believed in the false accusations made against General Yu Qian, who had once defended the capital, and had him executed. He trusted and rewarded Shi Heng and Cao Jixiang, who had supported his restoration. Shi was given the title of Lord Zhongguo and Cao became the head of protocol. Later, these two led unsuccessful rebellions from within the palace.

In April 1464 Zhu Qizhen fell terminally ill. In his will he made it clear that the crown prince would succeed him. Also he banned the institution of burying live attendants with the dead, ending this cruel practice which the Ming Dynasty had begun.

5. Emperor Daizong—Zhu Qiyu (1428-1457)

Zhu Qiyu was the half-brother of Yingzong. In 1449, following the "Incident of Tumubao," when Yingzong was captured by the Wala tribe, he was selected by the empress dowager to be the Prince Regent. In September of the same year he usurped the throne, calling his reign Jingtai. He was on the throne for eight years.

After Daizong became emperor he made Yu Qian his Minister of War. Through Yu's efforts, the Ming armies were once again strengthened. They repelled the frequent attacks on Beijing by the Wala troops, forcing the latter to negotiate a peace and return the captured Yingzong.

On Yingzong's return, Daizong placed him in the Southern Palace

Emperor Daizong

to prevent him taking power again. For Yingzong, this amounted to house arrest.

One night in the first lunar month of 1457 the already very sick Daizong heard chimes and drums sounding throughout the city. He sent a eunuch to investigate. When he learned that Yingzong had returned to the palace and seized power he could say nothing but "Good! Good! Good!"

On the following day he was placed under house arrest in the Western Palace. He died a few days later, at the age of 30. Some say he died of grief; others that he was tortured to death. His mausoleum, which had been built when he was alive, was destroyed at Yingzong's order. He was buried with his concubines in the Western Hills in a ceremony due to one with the rank of prince.

6. Emperor Xianzong—Zhu Jianshen (1447-1487)

The eldest son of Zhu Qizhen, Zhu Jianshen was granted the title of crown price. When daizong replaced Yingzong as emperor Zhu Jianshen was demoted to Prince Yi. After the restoration of Yingzong, however, his title of crown prince was restored.

In the first lunar month of 1464, when Yingzong died, Zhu Jianshen ascended the throne, and titled his reign Chenghua.

He became crown prince when he was six, and had always been served by a maid of honor named Wan. When he ascended the throne at the age of 16 he was still obsessed by the

Emperor Xianzong

then 35-year-old Wan and granted her the title of *guifei*, or highest-ranking imperial concubine. After the only baby son she gave birth to died not long after he was born, she allowed none of the other palace women to give birth to a child for the emperor. Whoever was pregnant would either be forced to abort the baby or be killed. When Zhu Jianshen reached middle age, he was sad that he did not have a son to succeed him. It was believed, however, that a boy born to another maid of honor and secretly raised in the Forbidden City was his son, and this boy later succeeded to the throne as Emperor Xiaozong.

During the reign of Xianzong the collaboration between the eunuchs and Wan led to the decline and corruption of the government. A ballad popular at the time best describes the situation: "The three grand councilors are like paper puppets. The six ministers are like clay figures." The three grand councilors refer to Liu Ji, Liu Xu, and Wan An, who had no abilities but were good at bragging and sycophancy. Wan An, the nephew of Wan, was a spy planted in the cabinet by his aunt. The six ministers were merely a group of sycophants who threw in their lot with Wan and the eunuchs. Xianzong, muddleheaded and a womanizer, was obsessed with Daoism and neglected his duties, making it difficult for the ministers to see him. He also relied on eunuchs.

In order to strengthen his rule, Emperor Xianzong had a force of secret police commanded by eunuch Wang Zhi. Wang would report to the emperor whatever he learned from the street gossip about political affairs, and he often persecuted the innocent, which made everyone, in and out of the government, feel threatened. A man who spent without restraint, Xianzong used up all the gold hoarded by his ancestors during his reign.

The death of Wan in the spring of 1487 was a heavy blow to Xianzong. He felt so sad he did not go to court for seven days. Shortly after her death, he also died, in August 1487.

7. Emperor Xiaozong—Zhu Youcheng (1470-1505)

The son of Xianzong, Zhu Youcheng was granted the title of

Emperor Xiaozong

crown prince in 1475. He ascended the throne in September 1487, one month after his father's death. In the following year he named his reign Hongzhi.

As the crown prince he had survived numerous persecutions by Wan and her group. Now that he was in power, he spared no effort to clear out the remaining confederates of Wan. Once, a whole basket of memorials to Xianzong by Wan An concerning sexual prowess was found. Thinking that such a grand councilor could not possibly assist him in running the country, Xiaozong dismissed him. He also declared that about 1,000 people including corrupt eunuchs and Wan An's relatives were guilty of offences and sent them into exile. At the same time, he reinstated some virtuous officials such as Qiu Jun, Xu Pu, Liu Jian, Xie Qian, and Li dongyang. He could also take advice from his subordinates. In his early days as emperor he wanted to have a pavilion set up on top of Wansui Hill so that he could sightsee from there. A student from the imperial college named Hu Chen sent a letter asking him not to do so. Everyone worried about what would happen to Hu Chen, but after Xiaozong read the letter he thought that Hu Chen's appeal was reasonable and, instead of declaring him guilty of an offense, he appointed him to the position of district magistrate in Yunnan. Xiaozong also ordered reductions in the amount of tributes, taxes and terms of penal servitude. At the same time, he ordered aid for victims of natural calamities. Under his rule which was characterized by stability and prosperity, the people enjoyed a peaceful life.

Emperor Xiaozong once became obsessed with superstition and his favorite was the eunuch Li Guang. After Li committed suicide he had Li's house searched, as he believed that the eunuch had some mysterious magic book. What was discovered, however, were piles of accounting records showing Li's corruption and bribery. This once again made him realize that he should distance himself from corrupt officials and befriend virtuous ones.

When he fell seriously ill in 1505 he summoned all the worthy officials to the Hall of Heavenly Purity and gave an order that the Crown Prince Zhu Houzhao was to succeed him after his death. "The prince is a smart boy," said the emperor. "But he is too young, and plays too much. I hope you will all assist him in government affairs so that he will be competent at his job. If you promise to do so, I can die at ease."

8. Emperor Wuzong—Zhu Houzhao (1491-1521)

Zhu Houzhao, the only son of Xiaozong, was given the title of crown prince in 1492. He ascended the throne in 1505, when Xiaozong died, and named his reign Zhengde. Unlike his father,

Emperor Wuzong

he trusted treacherous court officials and had a lust for women. He was said to be the most promiscuous and decadent emperor of the Ming Dynasty. He reigned for 16 years and died at the age of 30.

The lecherous Zhu Houzhao had secret chambers for his women, with whom he spent most of his time. When he got tired of the women within the palace, 12 women from what is today's Central and Western Asia were brought to him. But, not satisfied with the 12, he ordered all the women from the same area living in the houses of his officials brought to him as well. An official named Ma Ang took his married sister, who could sing and dance well, away from her husband and offered her to Emperor Wuzong. Ma Ang was immediately promoted because of this. Wuzong, being an alcoholic, often went to drink at Ma Ang's house. When he noticed that Ma Ang had a beautiful concubine, he took her away from him, which led to the promotion of two of Ma Ang's brothers. Sometimes, he would go out of the palace in plain clothes with his favorite eunuchs to look for beautiful women. When he spotted one he liked he would demand her favors, rousing the anger of the ordinary people.

In June 1519 Zhu Chenhao, the Prince of Ning led a rebellion, which was later supressed. Wuzong, who kept the news of the victory a secret, used this opportunity as an excuse to go on a southern expedition. All the way to Nanjing he constantly captured women. For fear of being taken by Wuzong, some women hurried to get married. He did not come back to Beijing from his "southern expedition" until the end of the following year. He became seriously ill soon after his trip and finally died in 1521.

Wuzong was also known for his ridiculousness. He once led his troops to inspect the border at Datong in the name of Zhu Shou. When 50,000 Tartar troops, led by their khan, came south to harrass the border, he himself went so far as to challenge the Tartar soldiers, who had by then withdrawn. Wuzong and his men only engaged in a minor clash with the Tartar rearguard. In the battle, 16 Tartars were killed, while the casualties on his side reached hundreds. Regardless, Wuzong thought he had won the battle, and even bragged about it to the court officials: "Do you know that I killed one enemy soldier with my own hands?" Most officials thought this improper, and submitted a joint letter asking him to stop doing this. Wuzong's response was to punish them by either having them arrested, beaten to death, or demoted or dismissed from office.

During his reign he put eight eunuchs, known as the "eight tigers" in important positions. With the emperor to back them up, they acted in a tyrannical way. They named 53 loyal officials as traitors and banished them. Court power was in their hands. All memorials to the emperor had to be first submitted to Liu Jin, one of the eunuchs, before it was submitted to Wuzong. Interested only in pleasure, Wuzong thought it a burden to read and sign documents, and left these chores to Liu Jin. A poorly-educated man, Liu always took the documents back home and asked his brother-in-law and Zhang Wenmian, a debased scholar, to handle them for him. At the time, there was a popular saying in the capital that besides Emperor Wuzong there was an emperor named Liu. This was a time when eunuchs ruled. In 1510 Liu Jin was executed for plotting a coup. Together with his bodyguards, Wuzong searched Liu's house and confiscated a large amount of jewelry.

Wuzong also adopted 100 sons, who were all given the surname Zhu and told to seize farmland to be used to build mansions for the emperor. Other corrupt officials favored by Zhu Houzhao included Qian Ning and Jiang Bin. Because of all this, politics in the mid-Ming Dynasty were in a mess.

9. Emperor Shizong—Zhu Houcong (1507-1566)

Zhu Houcong was the eldest son of Zhu Youyuan. As Emperor Wuzong did not have any son or brother it was decided after his

death that his cousin Zhu Houcong should succeed him. Zhu Houcong, known as Emperor Shizong in history, ascended the throne in 1521. In the following year he named his reign period Jiajing, and reigned for 45 years.

Zhu Houcong was determined to do something good for the country when he became emperor. He abandoned some policies of the previous court and dismissed corrupt officials and eunuchs. He also executed Jiang

Emperor Shizong

Bin. He ordered that the grain tax in areas stricken by natural disasters should be reduced and that women offered to him as gifts should be sent home.

Not long after, he decided to name his father *huangkao*, a title given to the father of an emperor. This, in the opinion of many ministers, however, did not conform to traditional teaching, according to which only Xiaozong was eligible to be named *huangkao*. Instead of listening to their advice, Zhu Houcong had the protesting ministers either killed or imprisoned. This incident is known to history as the "struggle over the great rite," and the result was that many honest ministers left office, giving corrupt officials an opportunity to sneak into important positions.

Shizong was superstitious and engaged in the pursuit of immortality. He neglected court affairs for almost 20 years, which made it possible for Yan Song, a corrupt minister, to be the power holder for as long as 17 years. As Yan Song and his son had the final say in all promotions, those who wished to be promoted would go to their mansion to offer gifts. Sometimes there were so many of them that they had to wait in a long line outside before they were allowed to go in. Politics became lax and the finances were exhausted. Besides, harassment by Japanese pirates along the southeast coast, invasion by Mongol troops and numerous peasant uprisings all added to the ever-intensifying social crises.

In his pursuit of immortality, Zhu Houcong even ordered that 300 girls under 14 years old and 100 girls under 10 be brought to the palace so that a so-called "elixir of life" could be extracted from their first periods. In addition, 1,000 girls were chosen from all over the country for Shizong's pleasure. According to the rules of the court, all women who had slept with the emperor would be given titles. As Shizong had slept with so many women he sometimes forgot to give titles to them, thus causing widespread resentment. In 1542, a group of palace ladies tried to assassinate the emperor. (See "Palace Ladies Try to Assassinate the Emperor")

At that time, an official named Hai Rui, known for his honesty, was made Minister of Revenue. When he realized how decrepit and muddleheaded the emperor was, Hai Rui parted from his wife and bought himself a coffin before submitting a memorial to the emperor. Shizong refused to come to his senses and threw Hai Rui into prison.

Contrary to his wish of becoming immortal, Shizong died in

December 1566, as a result of taking toxic "elixirs of immortality."

10. Emperor Muzong—Zhu Zaihou (1537-1572)

The third son of Shizong (Zhu Houcong), Zhu Zaihou, was given the title of Prince Yu in 1539, and succeeded to the throne in 1567, after the death of his father. In the following year he named his reign period Longqing.

Emperor Muzong

After his enthronement Zhu Zaihou severely punished the charlatan soothsayers in his father's employ and, at the same time, he adopted the suggestion by ministers Gao Gong and Zhang Juzheng that they negotiate peace with the Mongols. In addition, horse markets were opened in border cities to strengthen the ties between the Chinese and Mongols and help supply each other's needs, thus stabilizing the situation in the northern border regions. General Qi Jiguang was ordered to strengthen the defenses along the Great Wall. A general known for his strictness, Qi Jiguang was famed for his many military exploits.

Like his father, however, Muzong indulged in pleasure, and always had large groups of concubines waiting on him. He also spent freely and almost emptied the state treasury with his extravagance. In addition, there were frequent peasant uprisings throughout the country.

In March 1572 Muzong fell seriously ill. After two months' rest, he went back to court. Later, realizing that he would not live very long, he summoned his ministers Gao Gong, Zhang Juzheng and Gao Yi to his side and asked them to help the crown prince succeed to the throne. He died soon afterwards.

11. Emperor Shenzong—Zhu Yijun (1563-1620)

The third son of Muzong (Zhu Zaihou), Zhu Yijun, had shown himself to be clever at an early age. Once when he saw his father

riding a galloping horse he called out to him: "Father Emperor, you are the master of all under Heaven. It would be terrible if something happened to you if you rode too fast." He was only six when he said this. Muzong was pleased. He immediately dismounted and named him crown prince.

In 1572, when Muzong died, Zhu Yijun became emperor. In the following year he named his reign period Wanli.

Emperor Shenzong

As he was only ten years old when he succeeded to the throne the emperess dowager and his mother took care of government affairs. Later, Zhang Juzheng was named the First Grand Councilor and ran the government for almost a decade. As soon as he assumed office, Zhang rectified the administrative setup at all levels and strengthened the examination system. Economically, a policy known as the "One-Whip Method"—converting land rent and other taxes into silver and paying tax in accordance with the amount of land one owned—was adopted. He also advocated agricultural development. All these measures promoted social stability.

After the death of Zhang Juzheng, however, Emperor Shenzong indulged in wild debauchery, hoarded money and confiscated land. He had hundreds of women on call at any time. He drank excessively and he would kill anyone who displeased him. He built new imperial gardens and expanded the old ones. Every day, 30,000 soldiers and civilian craftsmen were mobilized to build his mausoleum, which took six years to finish. For 20 years Shenzong seldom went to court to discuss state affairs with his officials.

Memorials from ministers and his own instructions had to be conveyed by his eunuch attendants.

He was a man who loved money as much as his life. He also appointed large groups of eunuch officials as tax supervisors at mines all over the country, levying exorbitant taxes. All this resulted in a rising tide of anger and resistance among the people.

His wife, the emperess, did not give him a son, but he made one of her mother's maids pregnant. she gave birth to a boy, who was named Zhu Changluo and was to succeed to the throne.

In July 1620 Shenzong became ill and could not eat anything for two weeks. Knowing that he was going to die, he sent for Minister Zhang Weixian and asked him to assist the crown prince Zhu Changluo to govern the country. He died in the following month at the age of 58. He had reigned for 48 years.

12. Emperor Guangzong—Zhu Changluo (1585-1620)

The eldest son of Shenzong, Zhu Changluo was born to a maid of honor named Wang, who was promoted to the rank of concubine because of this.

In 1620, when Shenzong died, Zhu Changluo succeeded to the throne and named his reign period Taichang. Indulging in excessive pleasure, he died only 29 days after he had become emperor, at the age of 36.

Emperor Guangzong

Zhu Changluo was not his father's favorite when he was little. As Shenzong loved a concubine named Zheng, he always wanted to make her son the crown prince. His ministers, however, insisted that he follow the ancestral practice, which made it a rule that the eldest son be named crown prince. This was considered the "key to building the empire." The argument lasted for over a decade, and it was not until Zhu Changluo was 20 years old that his father reluctantly agreed to name him crown prince. This incident is known to history as the "Struggle over the Key to Building the Empire."

After Zhu Changluo was named crown prince the discontented concubine Zheng directed a plot later known as the "Case of the Club Attack," in which Zhu Changluo was nearly killed. (See "The Attempted Murder of a Crown Prince")

When Zhu Changluo became emperor, however, Zheng made an about-face, doing her best to win the new emperor's favor. She knew that the emperor was addicted to money and women, so she often went to visit him with jewelry and money as gifts. Besides, she also selected eight girls and sent them to him to be his maids of honor.

When Zhu Changluo was still the crown prince he already had many concubines and maidservants. Two of his maidservants who were known by the names of East Li and West Li were his favorites. Every day he spent almost all his time with these palace women, making his already poor health even worse. He could not even sit on the throne soon after he became emperor. He told his ministers that he felt dizzy and weak and could not walk.

When an official named Li Kezhuo learned of this, he offered the emperor some red-colored pills. The court ministers, however, insisted that Li take one pill himself before the emperor took one. Li suffered no ill effects, but Guangzong died on the morning of the following day after taking two pills. The "Red Pill Incident" remains a mystery. Together with the "Struggle for the Key to Building the Empire" and the "Case of the Club Attack," it helped to make the short reign of Guangzong a controversial one. These three incidents also reflected the acute struggle within the ruling class at the time.

13. Emperor Xizong—Zhu Youxiao (1605-1627)

Zhu Youxiao, the eldest son of Emperor Guangzong, ascended the throne after the death of his father in 1620. He named his reign

Emperor Xizong

Tianqi in the following year and reigned for seven years.

Zhu Youxiao became emperor when he was 15 years old. The maid-servant named West Li, who had once taken care of him when he was an infant, collaborated with a eunuch named Li Jinzhong (who later changed his name to Wei Zhongxian) in an attempt to manipulate the emperor. West Li even went so far as to live together with Zhu Youxiao in the Qianqing Hall (Hall of Heavenly Purity), the emperor's chambers. But she was later forced to move to another hall by the ministers Yang Lian and Zuo Guangdou.

Zhu Youxiao was brought up by a nanny named Ke, who was a promiscuous woman by nature. After the death of her husband she went to live with a eunuch named Wei Chao. Later, she gave up Wei Chao for another eunuch named Wei Zhongxian. Zhu Youxiao was 16 when he became emperor, while Ke was already 38 years old. Taking advantage of her access to the emperor, she seduced the emperor and was later given the title of Madame Fengsheng.

A lover of carpentry, Zhu Youxiao spent much of his time planing and sawing. He was so skilled that he even made a miniature Hall of Heavenly Purity. As a result of his obsession with carpentry, he neglected state affairs, giving opportunities for corrupt officials to stir up trouble. Collaborating with each other, Ke and Wei Zhongxian took charge of the government, and rode roughshod over anyone who opposed them. Wei Zhongxian, with the approval of Emperor Xizong, handled state affairs himself and put his trusted followers in key positions, leading to a situation in which eunuchs held the veins of power. Wherever Wei Zhongxian went he would always have hundreds of attendants crowding round him. During the reign of Xizong there were frequent peasant uprisings, foreshadowing the end of the Ming Dynasty.

Zhu Youxiao was also fond of dramatic performances. In summer he would dress up as if it were winter and pretend to carry out an inspection on a snowy night; or he would mount the stage and give a show. Once when he was rowing a boat he fell into the water. He caught a chill from which he never recovered, despite taking so-called "miraculous elixirs." Soon he contracted dropsy. Knowing that his days were numbered, he sent for his brother Zhu Youjian and made him heir to the throne. He was only 23 when he died in August 1627.

14. Emperor Sizong—Zhu Youjian (1611-1644)

The younger brother of Emperor Xizong, Zhu Youjian was the fifth son of Emperor Guangzong and the last Ming emperor.

Emperor Sizong

In 1627 he ascended the throne and was to reign for 17 years. He named his reign period Chongzhen.

In 1644, when Li Zicheng, the peasant leader, took Beijing, he hanged himself from a tree in what is today's Coal Hill Park. He was 34 years old.

Zhu Youjian was determined to get rid of the power group headed by Wei Zhongxian as soon as he ascended the throne. He ordered Wei Zhongxian banished to Fengyang in Anhui Province to guard the imperial mausoleum. Knowing that he was doomed, Wei hanged himself on the way to Fengyang. As for Wei's 262 closest followers, Zhu Youjian had them either executed, dismissed from office or otherwise punished.

Unlike his predecessors, he was a diligent emperor who attended to governmental affairs. Learning of a famine, he ordered economies to be undertaken in the Forbidden City in order to set an example.

Emperor Chongzhen was a suspicious person by nature, and this led to the unjust execution of General Yuan Chonghuan. Huang Taiji, the emperor of the Manchu dynasty, northeast of the Shanhaiguan Pass, saw General Yuan as the main obstacle to his invasion of the Central Plain. So in 1629 he leaked to a captured eunuch named Yang a fabricated story about a "secret agreement" between Yuan Chonghuan and Huang Taiji himself. Then he released Yang, who, not knowing that it was a trick, reported to Chongzhen what he had heard. Without checking, Chongzhen had Yuan Chonghuan arrested and executed. Also because of his distrustfulness, on an average, he had three grand councilors replaced every year during his 17-year reign period, which was unprecedented. It was no wonder that, despite his diligence, his paranoia and lack of judgment hastened the end of the 276-year-old Ming Dynasty.

15. Emperor Shizu—Fu Lin (1638-1661)

Shizu, or Aisin-Gioro Fu Lin, was the ninth son of Huang Taiji. He ascended the throne on the very day his father died, in August 1643. In the following year he named his reign period Shunzhi.

Fu Lin was six when he became emperor. His uncle Dorgon,

acting as regent, arrogated all powers to himself. Leading the Qing troops through the Shanhaiguan Pass, and finally to the occupation of Beijing, Dorgon was the chief leader in establishing the Qing Dynasty. He was later granted the title of prince regent. In 1651, when Dorgon died, Fu Lin took over government affairs. The first emperor of the Qing Dynasty to sit on the throne in the Hall of Supreme Harmony in the Forbidden City, Fu Lin reigned for 18 years. His death at

Emperor Shizu

24 was caused by his grief over the death of a favorite concubine.

When the Qing first entered the Central Plain they adopted a moderate policy to try to win over the remnants of the Ming Dynasty, who were still putting up resistance. But once they had gained a firm foothold, they ordered all Han men to follow the Manchu custom of shaving their foreheads and growing long pigtails. They threatened, "Either lose your hair or lose your head." Many people were in fact killed because they refused to follow this order. In addition, the Qing confiscated land and banned Han scholars from forming any kind of associations. In order to wipe out the Ming power in the south, Qing troops marched south and carried out savage massacres.

When Fu Lin learned, after the death of Dorgon, that the regent had once schemed to take power for himself, Fu Lin ordered that Dorgon's remains be exhumed and publicly flogged. All his family property was confiscated as well. From then on, Fu Lin demanded that all documents be forwarded to him, showing his determination to control the government himself.

Fu Lin encouraged farming, reduced taxes and severely punished corrupt officials. All these measures promoted the restoration and development of production. He was also eager to learn and was a talented painter.

Fu Lin was attracted by Buddhism. He went to study under Yulin, a master of the Zen doctrine, and gave himself the Buddhist name Xingchi. He wrote a poem later to express his intention at one time of becoming a monk. It read, "I regret my momentary slip,/ A dragon robe replaced my purple *kasaya*./ I was born a Buddhist monk,/ How did I end up in an imperial family?"

He was madly in love with Dong Eshi, his sister-in-law, and granted her the title of *fei* (concubine). Dong Eshi's death in 1660 saddened him so much that he expressed the wish to become a monk.

On January 6, 1661 Fu Lin went to court as usual. Then on the following morning he was reported to be dead. Yet his body was not seen by anyone. He left a will behind bequeathing the throne to Xuan Ye. It was believed that he had not actually died. Instead, he just gave up his throne and went to Mount Wutai, an area sacred to Buddhists, where he became a monk. The rumor had it that Emperor Kangxi actually visited his father there. This incident is one of the three major mysteries of the Qing Dynasty, the other two being "The Empress Dowager Marries the Emperor's Uncle" and "The Mystery of How Yongzheng Became Emperor." Nevertheless, experts deny the possibility of Shunzhi ever becoming a monk.

16. Emperor Shengzu—Xuan Ye (1654-1722)

Shengzu, or Aisin-Gioro Xuan Ye, was the third son of Emperor Shunzhi. He ascended the throne the day his father was supposed to have died. He named his reign Kangxi, a name that people

Emperor Shengzu

would use to refer to the emperor himself (as with other Ming and Qing emperors). He was on the throne for 61 years, making him the longest-reigning emperor in China's history. He died at the age of 69.

As Kangxi was only eight years old when he ascended the throne he was assisted by four ministers. One of the four, named Aobai, was a domineering person who quickly gathered all power into his own hands. He insisted on making all government decisions, paying scant attention to the emperor.

In 1667, when Xuan Ye was 14, he decided to take over the reins of government himself, and thus the power that belonged to him. Having tricked Aobai into thinking him harmless, Kangxi had him arrested. (See "How Emperor Kangxi Removed Aobai"). From then on, Kangxi became emperor in fact as well as in name.

Later, he put down the rebellion of the Three Feudatories and subdued Zheng Keshuang, the grandson of Zheng Chenggong, the conqueror of Taiwan, bringing China again under one rule. He ordered the Manchus to stop taking land from the Han people, built water projects and encouraged farming. He also organized the compilation of the 10,000-volume *Completed Collection of Graphs and Writings of Ancient and Modern Times* and the famous *Kangxi Dictionary*. Kangxi was one of the most influential emperors in the later period of China's feudal society. Under his reign China became one of the most powerful and unified empires in the world. The heyday of the Qing Dynasty under Kangxi and grandson Qianlong was to last into the 18th century.

An emperor of great achievements, Kangxi was very diligent and eager to learn. He even took foreigners as his teachers, who taught him Western science, technology, philosophy and customs.

Kangxi was a man of political insight and a shrewd judge of character. Ge Li, a viceroy in the south harbored a grudge against Chen Pengnian, prefect of Suzhou. He wrote to Emperor Kangxi, telling him that Chen had once written a poem that was intended as an attack on the emperor. After reading his letter and the poem, Kangxi did not see anything in Chen's poem that betrayed rebellious thoughts. He called his ministers together and criticized Ge Li for lodging a false accusation against Chen Pengnian. He told the ministers present that it was a trick played by a narrow-minded person and that no one should be fooled by it. Having said this, Kangxi showed Ge's letter and Chen's poem to everyone, making Ge Li very embarrassed. Kangxi did this to educate the other officials and to warn those with ulterior motives.

With 35 sons, Kangxi had a difficult task choosing his successor. At first, he decided he would let his eldest son succeed to the throne. Then he changed his mind. His indecisiveness gave opportunities to all his sons to intrigue for the throne. Eventually, it was Yin Zhen, the fourth son, who was granted the title crown prince. It was said that Longkeduo, Yin Zhen's uncle, who was in charge of the Beijing Garrison, took advantage of his easy access to Kangxi and secretly changed his will to enable Yin Zhen to mount the throne. (See "The Mystery of How Yongzheng Became Emperor")

17. Emperor Shizong—Yin Zhen (1678-1735)

Shizong, or Aisin-Gioro Yin Zhen, was the fourth son of Emperor Kangxi. He ascended the throne in 1722 after the death of his father. He named his reign Yongzheng.

Emperor Shizong

Shrewd and adept at scheming, after his enthronement Yongzheng had his brothers either killed or put under house arrest. He even found an excuse to execute General Nian Geng-yao who had assisted him in seizing the throne. His uncle Longkeduo was also put under house arrest as he knew too much about the inside story of the power struggle. Yongzheng was a man of such a vicious nature that it was said that he and his cronies invented an execution device in the form of a bag which was placed over the victim's head. Inside were fixed knives, and the bag could be mechanically manipulated so as to sever the head. In order to strengthen his personal power he set up a secret police division directly under his charge and placed it above the cabinet. To weaken the power of the heads of the banners he always had secret agents keeping a watch on them. He frequently searched the houses of officials and confiscated their property, for which he got the nickname "the house-searching emperor."

However, Yongzheng was a politically diligent emperor. Carrying forward Emperor Kangxi's military achievements, he put down border rebellions and reformed the tax system by levying taxes according to the amount of land one owned and abolishing the dual land tax-poll tax system, greatly reducing the burden on the poor and promoting production. As a result, the economy developed rapidly during the reign of Yongzheng.

Learning a lesson from Emperor Kangxi in selecting his successor, Emperor Yongzheng chose his without asking his ministers to discuss it. He wrote the name of the person he had chosen on two pieces of paper and hid one in a box which was put behind a horizontal inscribed board, and kept the other with him. So when the emperor died, the head eunuch was to take them out and read them out loud in front of everyone.

The story of the death of Yongzheng is full of suspicion. Yongzheng was an emperor who would imprison or execute an author for writing something that he considered offensive to himself. Lü Liuliang was a writer from Zhejiang. After his death, it was reported that his work contained anti-Qing ideas. Yongzheng ordered his grave opened, his corpse flogged and his works burned. In addition, he also had Lü's family members either put in jail or exiled. More than 1,000 people were involved. It was said that Lü's granddaughter, Lü Siniang, escaped. She went to learn martial arts and was determined to get revenge for her grandfather.

On the evening of August 23, 1735, when a eunuch realized that Yongzheng had been sleeping for a long time he became suspicious and went to report to the empress. She found that the emperor was dead. Legend has it that it was Lü Siniang who had managed to sneak into his chamber and killed Yongzheng.

Scholars, however, think it would have been impossible for a woman to sneak into the Forbidden City and assassinate the emperor. They argued that Yongzheng had suffered from some kind of disease for three months before he died.

Another rumor had it that since Yongzheng thought that he had consolidated his throne after getting rid of Longkeduo, who knew too much about the inside story of the power struggle he had started, he abandoned himself to debauchery. This did a lot of harm to his health. He also may have poisoned himself unwillingly by taking potions containing gold.

18. Emperor Gaozong—Hong Li (1711-1799)

Gaozong, or Aisin-Gioro Hong Li, was the fourth son of

Emperor Gaozong

Emperor Yongzheng. He ascended the throne in August 1735 after the death of his father, Yongzheng. He was the first person to be secretly made crown prince in China's history. After Yongzheng died the chief eunuch took out the secret instruction from the box from behind the horizontal inscribed board in the Hall of Heavenly Purity and read it out loud in front of all the ministers. The instruction read, "Hong Li, the fourth son of mine, is the crown prince and will succeed to the throne." Hong Li became emperor in the same month, and named his reign Qianlong in the following year.

Emperor Qianlong carried forward the cause of reunification from emperors Kangxi and Yongzheng, and cracked down on separatist activities in border regions, making China the most powerful and unified country in Asia. Qianlong was good at enlisting able men to work for him. A very talented man himself, he had literary accomplishments, especially in calligraphy. Even today, his poems and inscriptions can be seen in many places in the Forbidden City.

There are many stories about Qianlong, but the story about a woman called Xiangfei (Fragrant Concubine) is particularly popular. While wiping out a rebellion at Mount Tianshan in the far west the Qing troops captured a concubine of the tribe leader and took her back to the Forbidden City. Not only was she beautiful, even her sweat smelt fragrant, hence her name. Qianlong decided to take her as a concubine and treated her well. As she was a Muslim, he ordered a mosque built for her. Yet, Xiangfei sternly refused to be the concubine of Qianlong. When the maids of honor were asked to cajole her, she brandished a dagger at them, scaring them away. When the empress dowager learned of this, she sent for Xiangfei and said: "If you don't obey, what do you plan to do in the future?"

"I would rather die to show my innocence," replied Xiangfei.

The empress dowager agreed that she could kill herself. After Qianlong learned that Xiangfei had committed suicide he became seriously ill. Xiangfei's body was taken back and buried at Kashi, Xinjiang.

In recent years, however, many experts have cast doubt on the above story. In their opinion, Xiangfei was actually Concubine Rong of Emperor Qianlong. She was a Uygur and was 23 years Qianlong's junior. Emperor Qianlong loved her very much for her contribution to the unification of the country. She spent 28 years in the Forbidden City before she died at the age of 55 and was buried at the Eastern Qing Tombs.

Of all the emperors of the Qing Dynasty, Qianlong was the one who went to extremes in punishing people who he considered had written or said offensive things about him. When he considered that a sentence in a poem by Hu Zhongzao, a literatus from Hunan, was slanderous to the Qing Dynasty he ordered him and his whole family killed. Another story also tells how ready Qianlong was to find fault with people. One hot summer day Qianlong paid a visit to Ji Yun, compiler of the *Complete Library in the Four Divisions*. Ji Yun, a big man, did not like hot weather. With his pigtail coiled up and bare-chested, he was reading a manuscript when Qianlong arrived unexpectedly. Since he had no time to put on his clothes, he dived under his desk to hide from the emperor. Seeing this, Qianlong went to sit down. After a little while, thinking that the emperor had left, Ji Yun asked his attendants if the "old man" (In Chinese the expression is, literally "old head son") had left. When Ji realized that the emperor was still in the room he was struck dumb with fear. He started to kowtow to Qianlong and begged for forgiveness. "Why do you call me 'old man'?" asked Qianlong. "If you don't tell me the reason, your head will be removed on the spot!"

A very quick-witted man, Ji Yun answered, "I didn't make the name up; everyone in the city calls you that. Let me tell you why." He continued, "The emperor is also called 'ten thousand years.' Isn't that old? Since the emperor is above everyone, you are the head. Besides, the emperor is the son of Heaven, and that's why you are a son." Pleased at this, Qianlong warmed to Ji Yun and treated him reverently from then on.

Emperor Qianlong reigned for 60 years, only one year less than Kangxi, his grandfather. In order not to exceed the number of reigning years of his grandfather, he handed over the crown to his son, although he remained the power behind the throne until his death.

19. Emperor Renzong—Yong Yan (1760-1820)

Renzong, or Aisin-Gioro Yong Yan, was the 15th son of Emperor Qianlong. He ascended the throne in 1796, when his father abdicated and handed the crown over to him. He named his reign Jiaqing.

Although Yong Yan was now an emperor, he still had to be obedient to his father, and could not make any decision by himself. But as soon as his father died Emperor Jiaqing wasted no time in arresting He Shen, Qianlong's favorite minister, and confiscating

Emperor Renzong

from his house property worth one billion taels of silver—which equalled the total income of 20 years for the Qing government. He Shen turned out to be the biggest embezzler China had ever seen. He had kept 90 percent of the tribute sent to Qianlong for himself. Two weeks later He Shen was executed. All the confiscated property was taken by Emperor Jiaqing. A popular saying in those days went, "After He Shen fell, Jiaqing ate his fill." Jiaqing replaced He Shen's clique at court with a group of officials who had made brilliant achievements but whose career advancement had been blocked by He Shen.

Emperor Jiaqing was 39 years old when he took power in his own right, and he was eager to accomplish something. He ordered court expenses reduced, tribute exempted and southern inspection tours cancelled. Instead of changing his imperial robes for new ones, he would have them mended and wear them again and again. But corrupt politics, the high concentration of land in the hands of bureaucrats and landlords, and too many peasants losing their lands and homes contributed to the numerous peasant uprisings throughout the country during the rule of Jiaqing. The once-flourishing Qing empire under the rule of Kangxi, Yongzheng and Qianlong began to collapse. On February 20, 1803 a man named Chen De sneaked through the Shunzhen Gate of the Forbidden City and attempted to assassinate the emperor. A decade later rebellious peasants led by Lin Qing broke into the forbidden City. This incident really shocked Jiaqing, who ordered all the trees inside the Forbidden City cut down, as he believed they might provide cover for assassins. The later emperors did not plant any trees because of this. That is why few old trees can be seen in the forbidden City today.

During the 25 years of his rule Jiaqing did one thing which was praiseworthy; he banned the import of opium and severely punished opium smokers. He thought opium could "ruin life, and the consequence is as bad as poison."

In July 1820 Jiaqing went on a hunting trip at the imperial summer resort of Chengde. All of a sudden, he fell ill and never recovered. He summoned all his ministers to his side and told them that he had already chosen Min Ning—who happened to be at the summer resort at the time—to succeed to the throne. On July 25 Emperor Jiaqing died. He was 61 years old.

20. Emperor Xuanzong—Min Ning (1782-1850)

Xuanzong, or Aisin-Gioro Min Ning, was the fourth son of

Emperor Xuanzong

Emperor Jiaqing. He ascended the throne on July 25, 1820, the day his father died. He named his reign period Daoguang in the following year.

Emperor Daoguang had been keen on learning since his childhood, and was well educated. He was also known for his frugality. But his attempts to reform the government were blocked by venal officials, especially those in charge of river-harnessing projects. The "great banquet of the Manchu and Han cuisine" that would last three days and nights was created by these river project officials. For one pork dish they would kill dozens of pigs by slowly beating them with bamboo poles until they were dead. Then a small piece of tenderloin was cut off and the rest of the pig thrown away. A dish of goose's web required dozens to 100 geese. The geese would be put in a cage with a fire burning underneath a metal plate on which the geese stood. When they died the cooks would take the web and made the dish. A bowl of fish jelly would also require dozens of fish. Live carp would be beaten to death and their blood would be allowed to drip into boiling water to become blood jelly. (See *The Anecdotes of Yong An on the Luxurious Life Style of the River Officials*, by Xue Fucheng).

Unable to distinguish loyal from treacherous officials, Daoguang named Cao Zhenyong, an old and crafty bureaucrat, as grand councilor. When asked how to be a good official, Cao replied, "Just kowtow to the emperor and keep your mouth shut." After Cao died another wicked official, named Mu Zhang'a, became Daoguang's favorite. Wang Ding, an upright Han official, denounced Mu Zhang'a in front of Daoguang. Having a guilty conscience, Mu did not dare to say anything to defend himself. But Daoguang simply laughed and said to Wang: "You must be drunk," and told his eunuchs to send Wang Ding back home. On the following day Wang Ding, in spite of the danger of being excuted, went to see the emperor again and admonished him about Mu Zhang'a. Daoguang got so angry he stood up and tried to leave. Pulling the emperor's robe, Wang pleaded with him to dismiss Mu Zhang'a. But Daoguang still would not listen. After going back home, Wang Ding, doing what the ancients would have done in a situation like this, hanged himself. When Mu Zhang'a learned of this, he sent his men to Wang's home and told Wang's son, Wang Kang, not to tell the emperor the truth about his father's death, or he (Wang Kang) would lose his post. Yielding to this pressure, Wang Kang told the emperor that his father had died of illness. By doing this, he thought that he would be able to keep disgrace away from his family.

The Opium War broke out during the rule of Emperor Daoguang. He dismissed upright officials such as Lin Zexu and Deng Tingzhen, who wanted to resist the invaders, while giving important assignments to the corrupt Mu Zhang'a and Qi Shan. His adoption of a capitulation policy and hesitance on critical issues led to China's defeat. As the imperialist powers forced the Qing government to cede territory and pay indemnities, China was reduced to the status of a semi-colony.

In his later years Daoguang was indecisive about whether his fourth son, Yi Zhu, or his sixth son, Yi Xin, should be given the title of crown prince. One day, before Daoguang went on a hunting trip with his sons, Yi Zhu's tutor, Du Shoutian, told Yi Zhu that he should just sit there watching his brothers, and that he and his attendant, Qian Qi, should not fire even one shot. If the emperor questioned him about his behavior Yi Zhu should tell the emperor what Du had told him.

Yi Zhu did as his tutor told him; he sat there for the whole day without taking any active part in the hunting.

In the evening, when they returned from hunting, everyone except Yi Zhu, had something to show for the day's sport. Emperor Daoguang was enraged and rebuked Yi Zhu. Remembering what his tutor had told him, Yi Zhu said, "Now that spring is here and the birds and animals are pregnant with their babies, I just don't have the heart to hurt them. Besides, I don't want to compete with my brothers."

Hearing this, Daoguang was delighted. "You seem to have a very benevolent and generous heart," he said. "You could become a good monarch and run the country well." Later, Emperor Daoguang wrote Yi Zhu's name on a piece of paper and put it in a box where the name of the successor secretly selected by the emperor was supposed to be found. In the first lunar month of 1850, when Daoguang died, the piece of paper was taken out of the box, and was found to read, "Yi Zhu, the fourth son of the emperor."

Daoguang, who ruled for 30 years, died at the age of 69.

21. Emperor Wenzong—Yi Zhu (1831-1861)

Wenzong, or Aisin-Gioro Yi Zhu, was the fourth son of Emperor Daoguang. He ascended the throne in the first lunar month of 1850, when Daoguang died. In the following year he named his reign period Xianfeng.

Emperor Wenzong

There is another story about how Yi Zhu was chosen as the crown prince. Daoguang, unable to make up his mind between Yi Zhu, his fourth son, and Yi Xin, his sixth son as crown prince, sent for them for an interview. Before the interview, Zhuo Biantian, Yi Xin's tutor, said to Yi Xin: "If the emperor asks you a question, you should tell him all you know without any reserve." Du Shoutian, Yi Zhu's tutor, however, had better ideas. "You don't know as much as your brother when it comes to state affairs," said

Du, "so the best thing to do is, when the emperor mentions his poor health and tells you that he won't be on the throne for long, you should start to cry to show your affection, respect and loyalty." Yi Zhu did as he had been told, and, sure enough, Emperor Daoguang was impressed by what he thought was the boy's filial piety and decided to grant him the title of crown prince.

When the 20-year-old Yi Zhu ascended the throne, unlike Emperor Yongzheng, who killed his brother who had struggled with him for the title of crown prince, he granted his brother Yi Xin the title of Prince Gong and made his other brothers heads of prefectures. He also abandoned Daoguang's practice of excluding people of the Han nationality from high posts and put some Han officials in important positions. Not long after Xianfeng became emperor, however, the Taiping Revolution and the Second Opium War broke out. He relied on Zeng Guofan, a Han landowner, and others to suppress the Taipings, but toward the foreign invaders he adopted a policy of reconciliation, and signed the *Treaty of Tientsin* and the *Treaty of Peking*, pushing China into the position of being a semi-colonial society.

Emperor Xianfeng started to select pretty women to be his concubines in the year following his enthronement. A coquettish girl named Lan'er from the Yehenara Clan, who sang well, became Xianfeng's favorite. It was this girl who was to become the Empress Dowager Cixi. Xianfeng also abandoned the ancestral practice that allowed only girls from families of Manchu and Mongolian officials to become concubines. Four Han women with the names of Peony Spring, Apricot Flower Spring, Martial Forest Spring and Crabapple Spring, known as the "four spring girls," were lodged in the picturesque Palace of Perfect Purity (the old Summer Palace).

In September 1860, before the British and French allied troops attacked Beijing, Emperor Xianfeng escaped to the summer resort at Chengde along with over 100 of his family and concubines. The entourage included Empress Ci'an, Lady Yehenara and the "four spring girls."

Not long afterwards, the allied troops occupied Beijing and

looted the old Summer Palace before they burned it to the ground. The Qing court once again ceded territory and paid indemnities to the foreign invaders in return for peace. Despite all this, Xianfeng still did not dare to come back to Beijing. Instead, he spent his time in idleness and debauchery, making his already poor health worse. In July 1861 Xianfeng died of illness at the summer resort.

Just before he died he sent for the eight senior ministers and asked them to help the young prince to rule. Sensing the political ambition of Lady Yehenara, Xianfeng wrote a secret instruction to Empress Ci'an, telling her that if Yehenara tried to dominate the prince, who was her son, the empress was authorized to deal with her in accordance with the ancestral rules.

Xianfeng ruled for 12 years, and died at the age of 31.

22. Emperor Muzong—Zai Chun (1856-1875)

Muzong, or Aisin-Gioro Zai Chun, was the first son of Emperor Xianfeng and the woman who was to become Empress Dowager Cixi. He ascended the throne right after the death of his father in July 1861, and named his reign period Qixiang. As he was only six

Emperor Muzong

years old at his enthronement he had to be assisted by the eight senior ministers. A woman with strong political ambitions, Empress Dowager Cixi wanted to hold court herself, sitting behind a screen, which was opposed by leading ministers on the ground that "there was no such precedent in the Qing Dynasty." Realizing that fighting openly would not work, Cixi started to act secretly. She pretended to have a row with her trusted subordinate, the eunuch An Dehai, and ordered him sent to Beijing to be dealt with. An Dehai arrived in Beijing with a secret letter from Cixi to Yi Xin, asking him to hasten to Chengde on the pretext of attending Xianfeng's funeral. Yi Xin, who had obtained the backing of foreign powers by selling the country's sovereignty, and whose power was increasingly expanding, had made enemies among the top ministers, led by Sushun. When Yi Xin arrived at Chengde and met Cixi, they plotted a coup. Yi Xin returned to Beijing and drew Shengbao, who controlled the army, to his side. Together they took power. It was decided that Cixi and Ci'an would hold court from behind a screen. In the following year the title of the reign was changed to Tongzhi.

In name, both Cixi and Ci'an controlled state affairs, but as Ci'an was not interested in politics, power was in the hands of Cixi alone. The Empress Dowager suppressed the Taipings and the Nian rebels, temporarily relieving the crisis of the Qing government. The Self-Strengthening Movement, represented by Yi Xin, Gui Liang and Wen Xiang at the central government level and Zeng Guofan, Li Hongzhang and Zuo Zongtang at the local government level was initiated to introduce foreign military and industrial technology. This period is known as the "restoration of Emperor Tongzhi."

Emperor Tongzhi frequented brothels in the southern part of the capital, and eventually caught a venereal disease. There was a popular rhyme at the time that went, "As he preferred wild chicks to family ones, the poor Son of Heaven caught syphilis."

Tongzhi had been emperor for 14 years before he died in 1874, when he was only 19 years old.

23. Emperor Dezong—Zai Tian (1871-1908)

Dezong, or Aisin-Gioro Zai Tian, was the son of Prince Chun and the sister of Empress Dowager Cixi. When the heirless Emperor Tongzhi died in 1874 Cixi decided that her nephew Zai Tian should succeed to the throne, and in the following year named his reign period Guangxu.

Cixi's decision to make her nephew emperor was opposed by many ministers. Wu Kedu, an imperial censor, admonished Cixi at the cost of his own life. Before he went to see her, he took a large

Emperor Dezong

dose of opium. At the court he hectored Cixi as follows, "You chose Zai Tian just because he is the son of your sister, so that you can continue to dominate the court from behind the screen and keep power in your own hands." He continued, "I know you will try to inflict the worst tortures on me for what I have dared to say. But I've taken a lethal dose of opium, and I'm going to die soon. I just want you to know that all the people in the country will hate you for choosing Zai Tian as emperor." Having said this, he ran to the grave of Emperor Tongzhi and dropped dead. Cixi, of course, went ahead with her plan.

When Guangxu first took over the reins of government at the age of 17 he determined to make the country prosper through reform with the support of reformers at court. But during the "Reform Movement of 1898" he alienated the conservatives, including Cixi. Together with her lover, conservative minister Rong Lu, Cixi fashioned a conspiracy against Guangxu. They planned to stage a coup during Guangxu's review of the New Army in Tianjin. The plot was betrayed to Guangxu, however, and he notified Kang Youwei, Liang Qichao and Tan Sitong, the three leading reformers. After some discussion, they decided to send Tan Sitong to ask Yuan Shikai, commander of the New Army, to kill Rong Lu and arrest Cixi during the review. Yuan expressed his loyalty to the emperor and his support for reforms, but as soon as Tan Sitong had left Yuan reported what he had said to Rong Lu, who went to see Cixi at the Summer Palace. Together they hastened back to the Forbidden City. Cixi put Guangxu under house arrest. Kang Youwei and Liang Qichao managed to escape abroad, but Tan Sitong and five other reformers were executed. The "Reform Movement of 1898" had failed.

Guangxu wrote in his diary in October 1908: "I'm seriously ill. But I have the feeling that Cixi will die before me. If this is the case, I'm determined to have Yuan Shikai and Li Lianying executed."

Li Lianying managed to obtain this diary, and showed it to Cixi, who vowed that she would never die before Guangxu.

On October 21, 1909 Cixi ordered Li Lianying to "take care" of Guangxu's diet and health. Guangxu's health deteriorated on that very afternoon, and he died soon afterwards. Some say it was Cixi who ordered him poisoned; others say it was Yuan Shikai, who was afraid of being reprimanded by Guangxu. Recently, however, historians have argued that Guangxu died of lung failure. Cixi died only two days after Guangxu, on the evening of October 23.

Although Guangxu was on the throne for 34 years he was never able to give free play to his political ambitions. He was 38 years old when he died.

24. The Last Emperor—Pu Yi (1906-1967)

Aisin-Gioro Pu Yi was the last emperor in Chinese history. On October 20, 1908, when Guangxu was on his deathbed, his nephew Pu Yi was summoned to the palace by Empress Dowager Cixi.

The Last Emperor—Aisin-Gioro Pu Yi

When Guangxu died on the following day the three-year-old Pu Yi succeeded to the throne. His father, Prince Regent Zai Feng, and Empress Dowager Longyu, held the regency. In the following year, the reign period was named Xuantong.

When the Revolution of 1911 broke out a provisional government headed by Sun Yat-sen was founded in Nanjing on January 1, 1912. The imperial court was forced to issue an abdication edict in the name of Empress Dowager Longyu on behalf of

Pu Yi.

Pu Yi had been on the throne for only three years before the Qing Dynasty came to an end. Thanks to the preferential treatment granted to the imperial court by the provisional government, Pu Yi was allowed to reside in the three rear palaces in the Forbidden City together with a group of concubines and eunuchs. Princes, dukes and ministers, who wore pigtails and hats with red tassels, still kowtowed to the emperor. It was in the Forbidden City that Pu Yi spent his childhood and youth. It was also here that he, in accordance with imperial protocol, crowned his empress, conferred titles on his concubines and held a grand wedding ceremony in the Palace of Earthly Tranquility.

Pu Yi was influenced by modern trends. Despite strong opposition from those around him, he had his pigtail cut off. He ordered a telephone and a bath tub installed in his chambers, as well as fashionable sofas. He rode bicycle in the palace, and bought cars and hired cooks to make Western food for him. He lived a leisurely and carefree life until he was finally driven out of the Forbidden City.

In that time, however, there were still quite a few people who stubbornly defended the rule of feudalism. In June 1917, five years after the abdication of Pu Yi, warlord Zhang Xun took his army to Beijing, and in collaboration with the reformer-turned-royalist Kang Youwei, staged a farce of restoring the Qing Dynasty. With the support of these restorationists, Pu Yi announced his re-enthronement, before he was forced to announce his abdication once again in December.

On November 5, 1924 General Lu Zhonglin from warlord Feng Yuxiang's army took his troops to the Forbidden City and forced Pu Yi to leave immediately. Pu Yi left in a hurry and then stayed at the Northern Mansion as a guest of Prince Zai Feng.

Later, Pu Yi fled to the Japanese legation, and was escorted by the Japanese to Tianjin, where he continued his restoration activities.

On March 1, 1932 Pu Yi, with the support of the Japanese

became the "executive" of the bogus "Manchukuo empire." In 1934 he changed his title to "emperor" and named his reign Kangde.

In 1945, when the Japanese surrendered, Pu Yi announced his abdication and was then arrested by the Soviet Red Army and imprisoned. In 1950 Pu Yi was transferred to China and was sent to Fushun Prison for reform. In 1959 he was released on special pardon and returned to Beijing. He was assigned a job in the Beijing Botanical Garden, and in 1961 he became a literary and historical worker for the Historical Material Commission of the National Committee of the Chinese People's Political Consultative Conference (CPPCC), and later, a member of the Fourth National Committee of the CPPCC.

He died of illness on October 16, 1967.

Appendix

1. Emperors of the Ming Dynasty

Name	Title of Reign	Reign Period	Relation to Previous Emperor
Zhu Yuanzhang (Taizu)	Hongwu	31 (1368-1398)	
Zhu Yunwen (Gongmin)	Jianwen	4 (1399-1402)	grandson
Zhu Di (Chengzu)	Yongle	22 (1403-1424)	uncle
Zhu Gaochi (Renzong)	Hongxi	1 (1424-1425)	son
Zhu Zhanji (Xuanzong)	Xuande	10 (1426-1435)	son
Zhu Qizhen (Yingzong)	Zhengtong	14 (1436-1449)	son
Zhu Qiyu (Gongren Kangding)	Jingtai	7 (1450-1456)	younger brother
Zhu Qizhen (Yingzong)	Tianshun	8 (1457-1464)	older brother
Zhu Jianshen (Xianzong)	Chenghua	23 (1465-1487)	son
Zhu Youcheng (Xiaozong)	Hongzhi	18 (1488-1505)	son
Zhu Houzhao (Wuzong)	Zhengde	16 (1506-1521)	son
Zhu Houcong (Shizong)	Jiajing	45 (1522-1566)	cousin
Zhu Zaihou (Muzong)	Longqing	6 (1567-1572)	son
Zhu Yijun (Shenzong)	Wanli	48 (1573-1620)	son
Zhu Changluo (Guangzong)	Taichang	One month	son
Zhu Youxiao (Xizong)	Tianqi	7 (1621-1627)	son
Zhu Youjian (Sizong)	Chongzhen	17 (1628-1644)	younger brother